BLUE WILLOW PATTERN
COLLECTING THE UNUSUAL

HELSA MORGAN BOOKS

6 SMYTH PLACE, HAMILTON 3200

NEW ZEALAND

FIRST EDITION

PUBLISHED IN NEW ZEALAND IN 2017

A CIP CATALOGUE RECORD FOR THIS BOOK IS AVAILABLE FROM

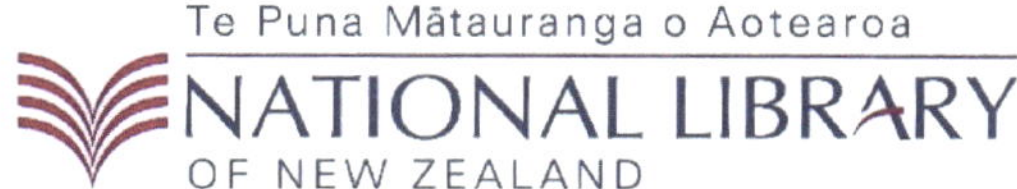

ISBN 978-0-473-39648-0

ALSO BY HUGH SYKES

ADVERTISING A TO Z FEATURING THE BLUE WILLOW PATTERN

PARTS 1 & 2

BOOKS HELD AT

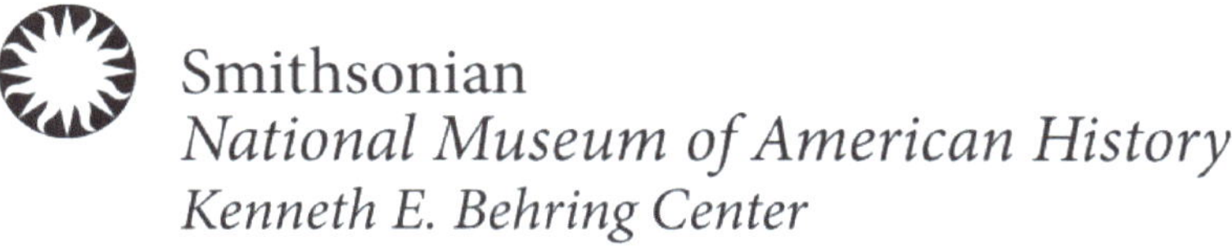

TYPESET 10/14 POINT BERLIN SANS FB

PRINTED AND BOUND IN AUCKLAND , NEW ZEALAND BY

BookPrint.

For additional copies of this book and my two previous books
Advertising A to Z Featuring The Blue Willow Pattern Parts 1 & 2,
please visit www.redwillow3.wix.com/book

INTRODUCTION

After writing two books which look at how the Blue Willow Pattern has been used in all forms of advertising to promote goods and services, I looked at our collection with my wife Kathy and realized that we have another story to tell. Many people around the world when they look around their home will probably find that they have something with the Blue Willow Pattern on it. When I say something, I mean something other than a piece of ceramic china showing the Blue Willow Pattern in its traditional blue and white. In this book you'll see how the Blue Willow Pattern has been used on numerous items that can be found in every room of a typical home. Many of the items to varying degrees have a practical use, these range from the everyday use of modern pots and pans to refined silver cutlery which might only be used for special occasions. Conversely quite a few items have a novelty value, but that said, in one example, the actual item such as a plant pot in the shape of a cat decorated in the Blue Willow Pattern can be used for its intended purpose.

The use of the Blue Willow Pattern to decorate all manner of items is not a recent phenomenon, while in this book you'll see plenty of modern day items, there are quite a few over 100 years old. A favorite of mine is a silver case made for holding gold sovereigns, the case which bears British hallmarks is dated 1912.

Often regarded as the oldest modern day pattern and America's favorite pattern, use of the Blue Willow Pattern can be found on every continent of the world. I'm not brave enough to say that the pattern has been produced in every country, but I can say with confidence that is has been produced by most countries. Perhaps I'll get around to writing a book on this in the future. In the meantime, there are plenty of Blue Willow Pattern items to consider just from the following countries, New Zealand, USA, Britain, Canada, Japan and Australia.

As with my first two books, I have received pictures and information from many Blue Willow Pattern collectors from all around the world.   All of these contributors are members of a group known as International Willow Collectors "IWC" for short. As the name suggests, IWC is a group of people who collect and learn all things about the Blue Willow Pattern. For further information about the IWC visit www.willowcollectors.org There you will find details about the club and local groups across the USA and New Zealand, additionally information about annual conventions held in July of each year are noted. At the time of print these are Atlanta 2017, Nashville 2018 and Dayton 2019.

Like my first two books, once you start looking for items to include in your books, you start finding more and more, particularly when word gets around that a book is being written. There is a very good chance that you'll have an unusual Blue Willow Pattern item in your possession that is not featured in this book, if this is the case then feel free to visit my website mentioned below and contact me. There is every possibility that I'll do a follow up book.

In this book I have taken a representative sample of particular items when there have been many to picture.

My first two books have been enjoyed by readers and collectors from all around the world. Additionally they are also held by several universities around the world and the Smithsonian. I hope you find this book interesting.

For further information and to leave comments please visit www.redwillow3.wix.com/book

Hugh Sykes

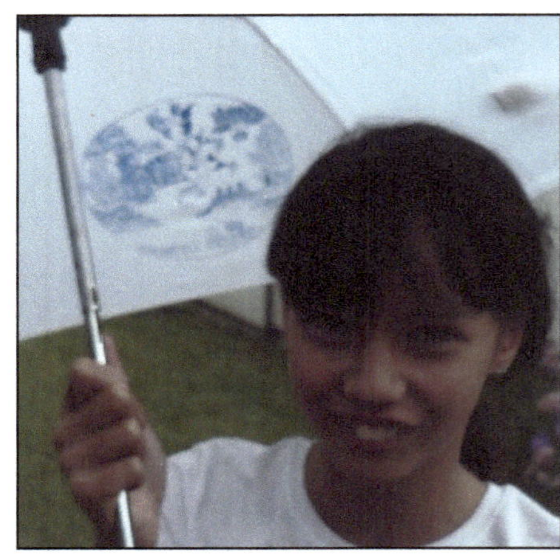

Even my daughter Sarah gets into the book by posing with an umbrella which just happens to show the Blue Willow Pattern on it.

CONTENTS

ADVERTISING

It just happens that as headings go alphabetically Advertising comes up first in this book. While many readers will have seen my first two books which were all about how the Blue Willow Pattern has been used to advertise goods and services, I thought it would be good to have at least one page in this book dedicated to Advertising, though you'll find more examples on other pages in this book.

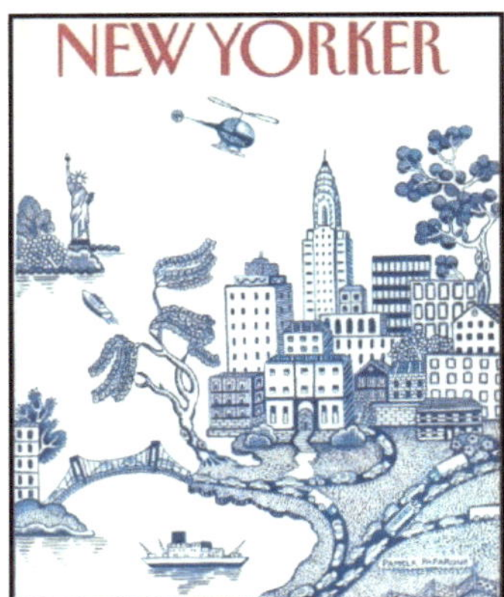

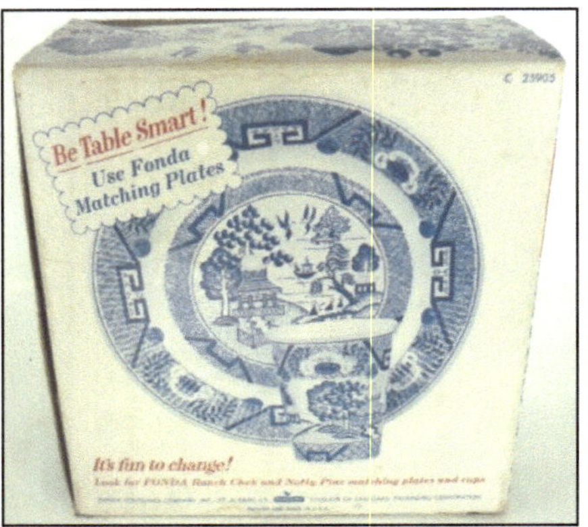

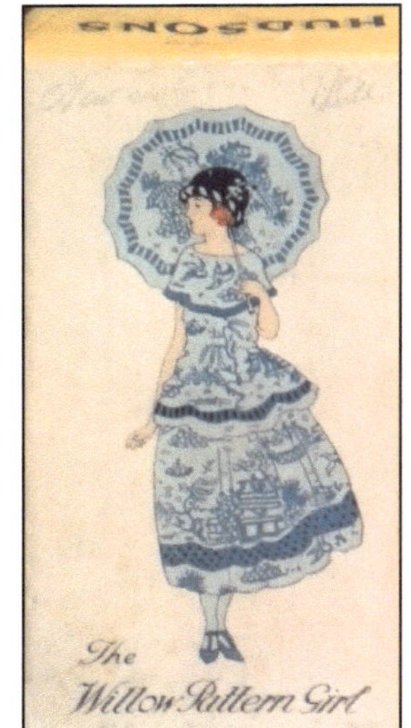

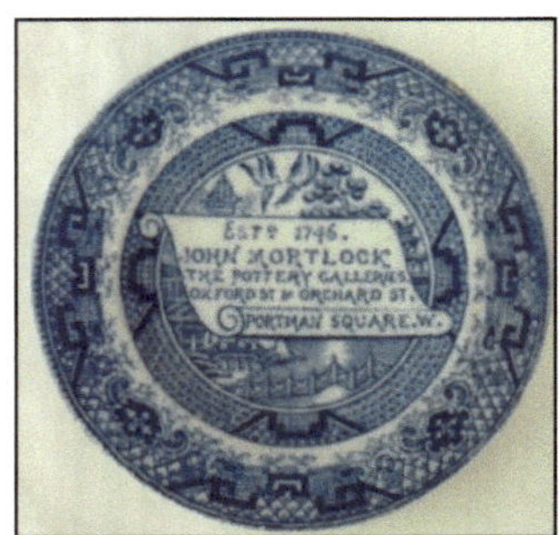

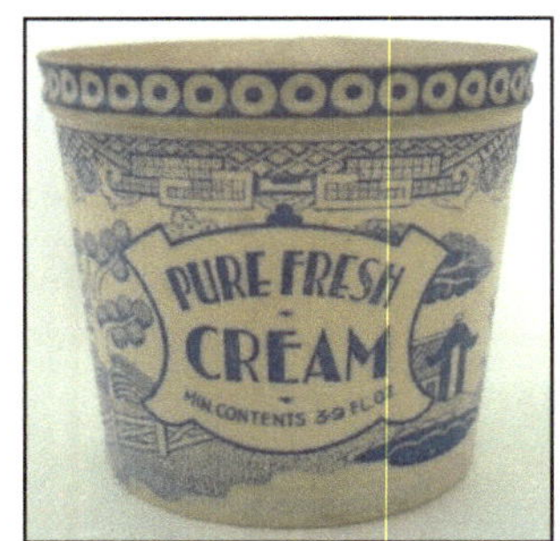

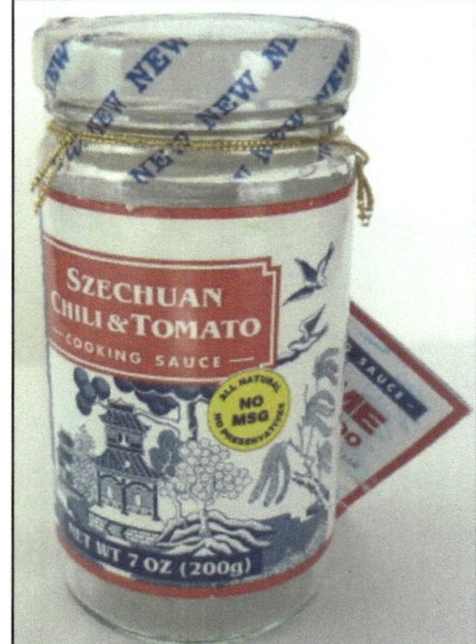

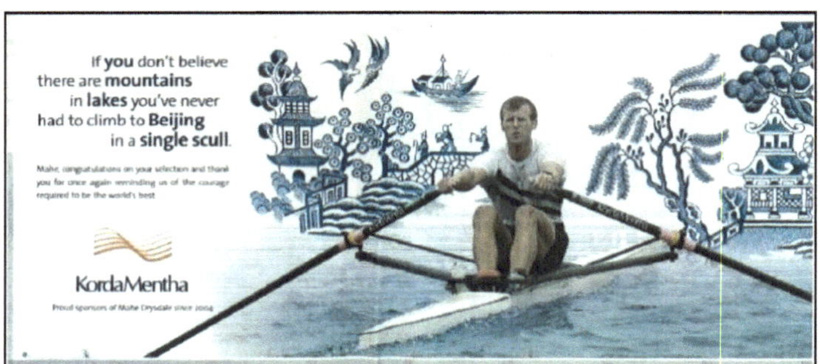

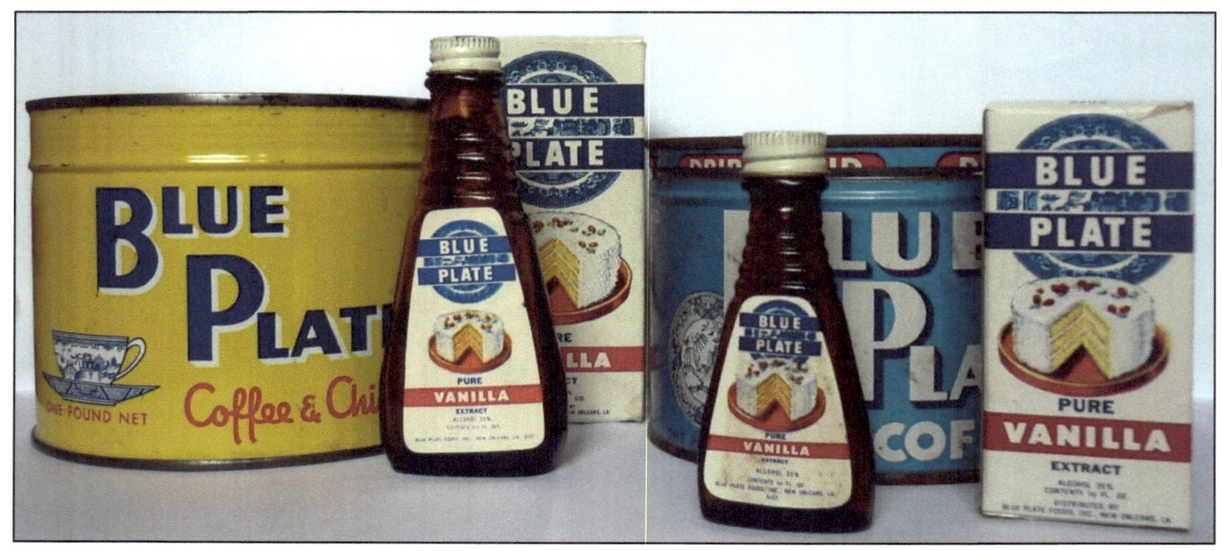

ANIMALS

In this book I have already dedicated pages to particular animals that bear the Blue Willow Pattern. The use of the word bear is quite appropriate as there are two bears on this page. One quite happy and jolly bear has a use as a money box, the other works out as a hook which can be fixed to a wall. The bears on this page are joined by some pigs who both enjoy being money boxes and a rabbit who not to be left out is a money box as well. On the centre row are a pair of elephants, these are novelty items and are part of a larger herd, with each member of the herd featuring one aspect of the Blue Willow Pattern. A cow creamer features on the bottom row made by Burleigh which is a milk jug.

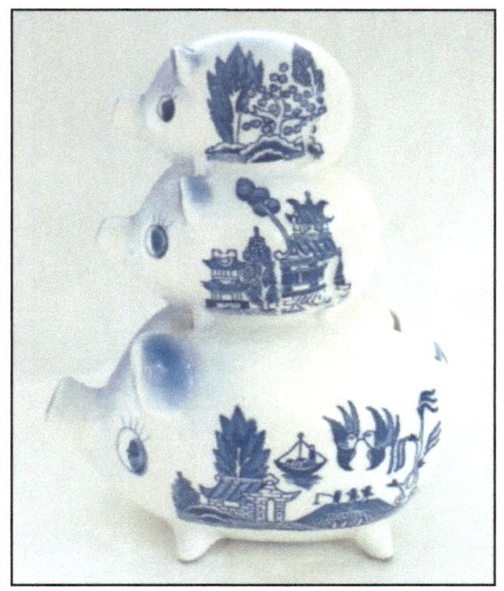
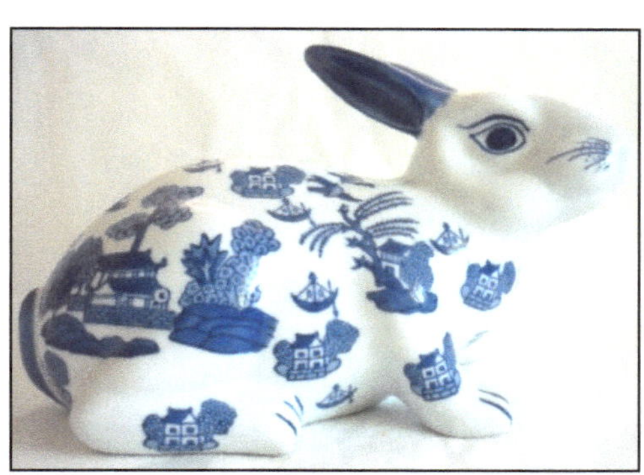
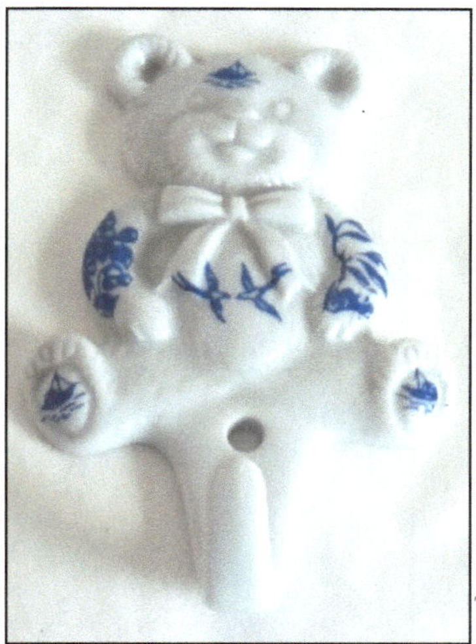

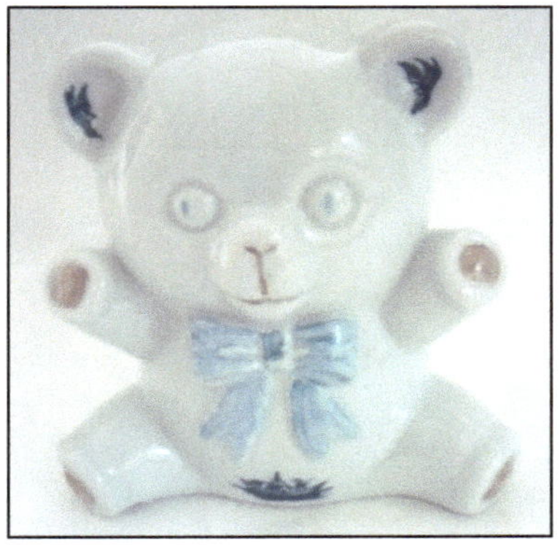
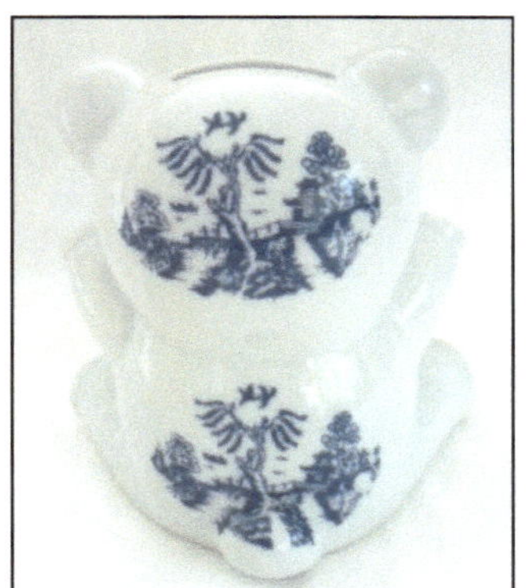
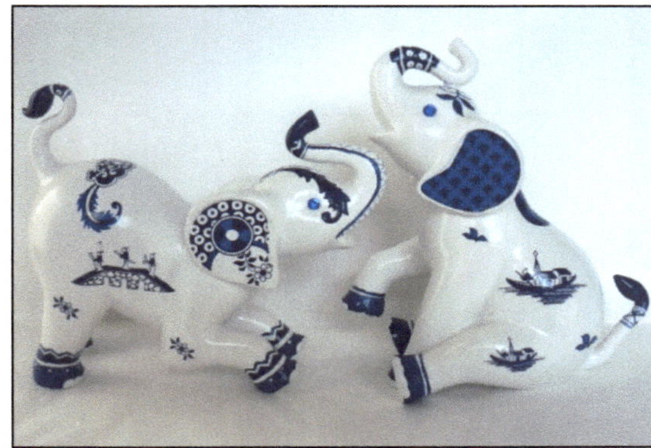

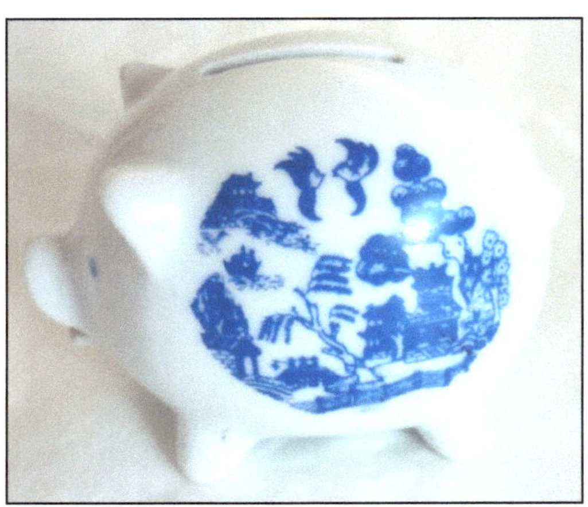
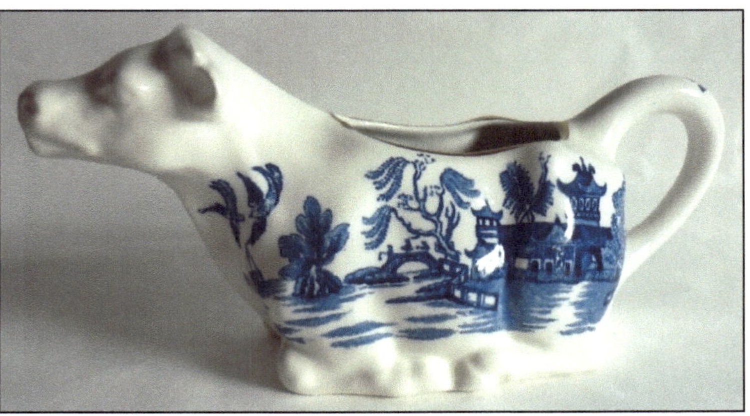

ASHTRAYS & SMOKING

Ever since 1492 when Christopher Columbus brought back the first tobacco leaves from the New World to Spain, it was inevitable that all sorts of paraphernalia would be created to go with the activity of smoking tobacco leaves. Of course with paraphernalia why have it plain when you can use the Blue Willow Pattern. If you have read my books on Advertising Featuring The Blue Willow Pattern, you'll see that ashtrays were commonly used to advertise goods, some of these are pictured below. On this page you'll also see some cigarette lighters and a matchbox cover.

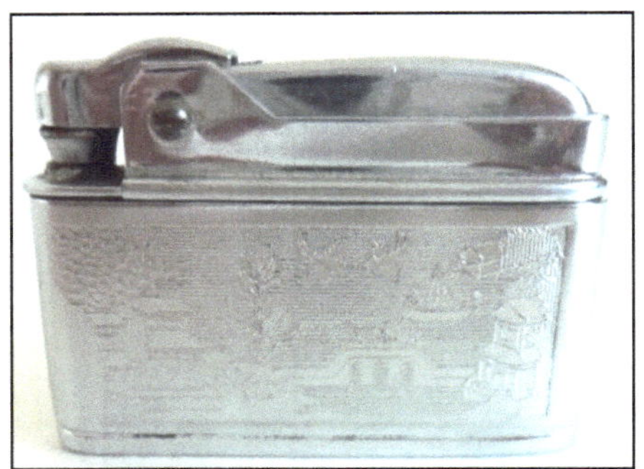
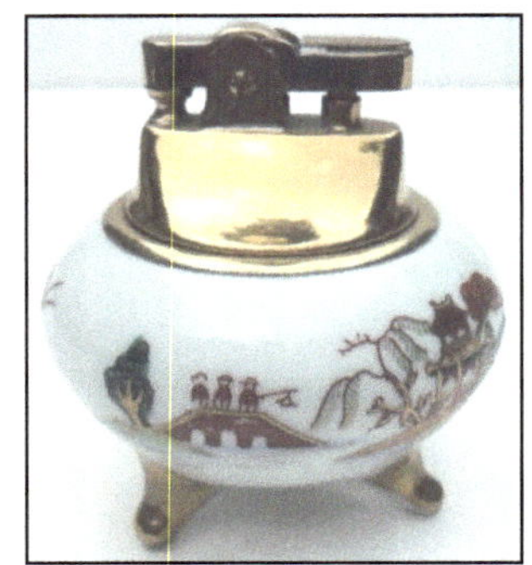
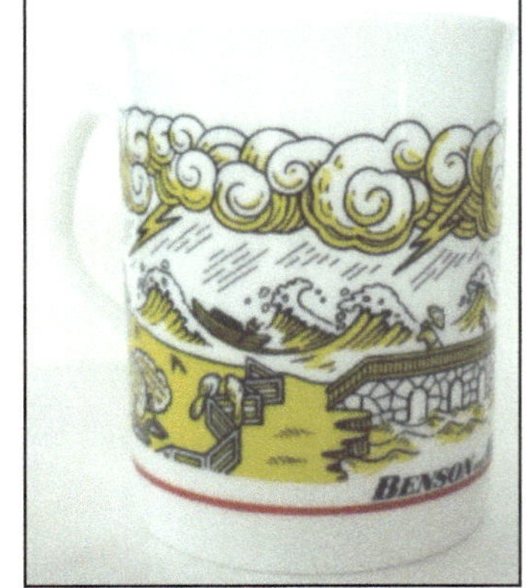

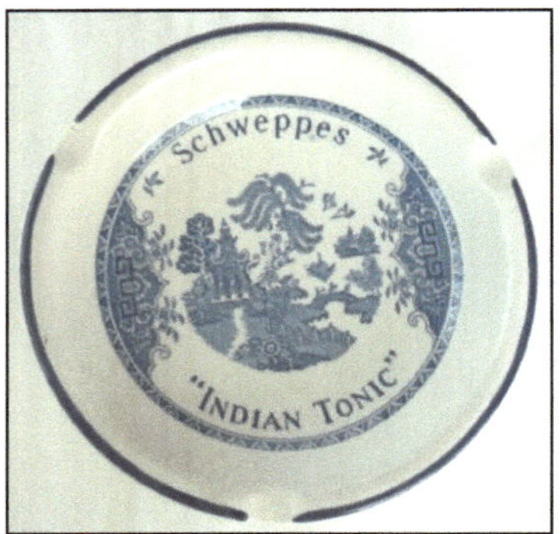

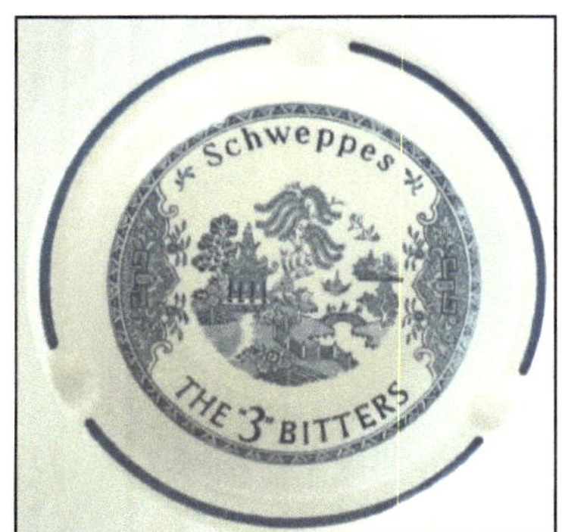

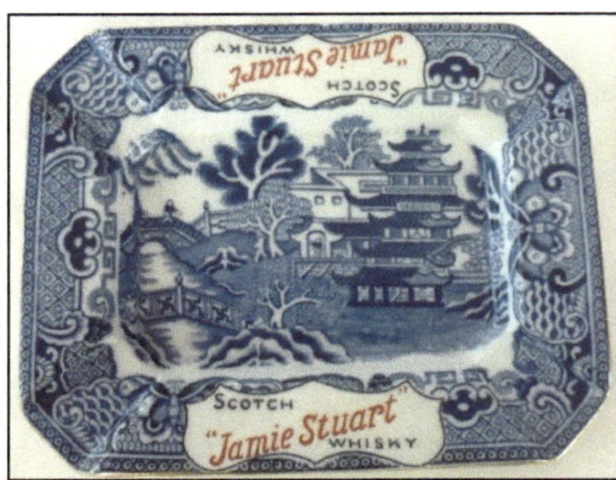

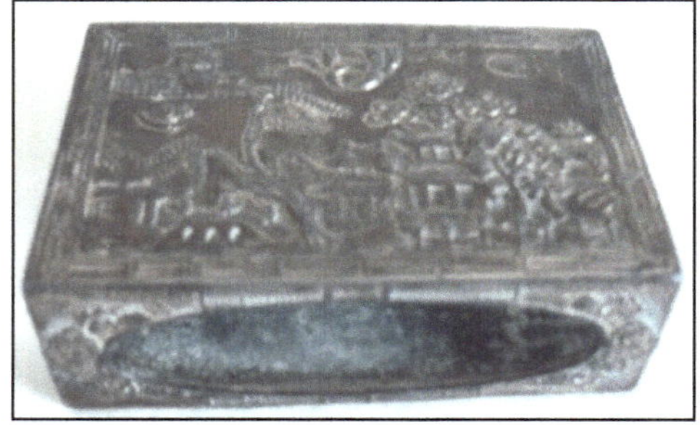

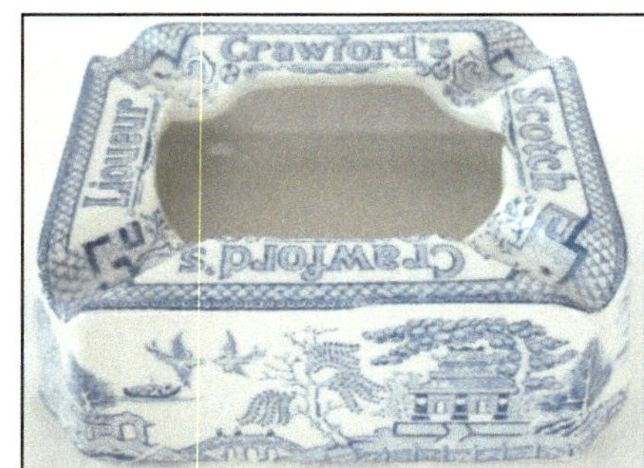

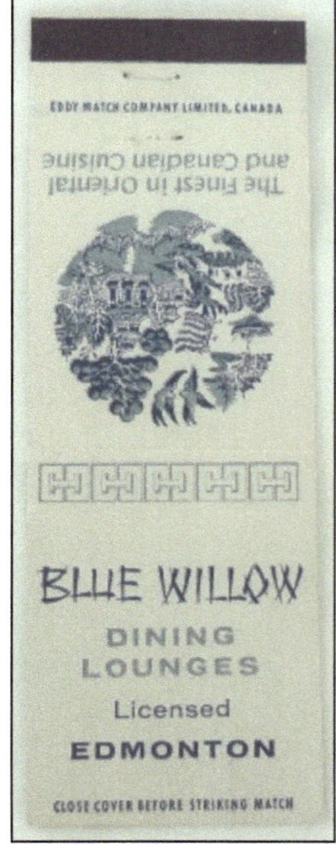

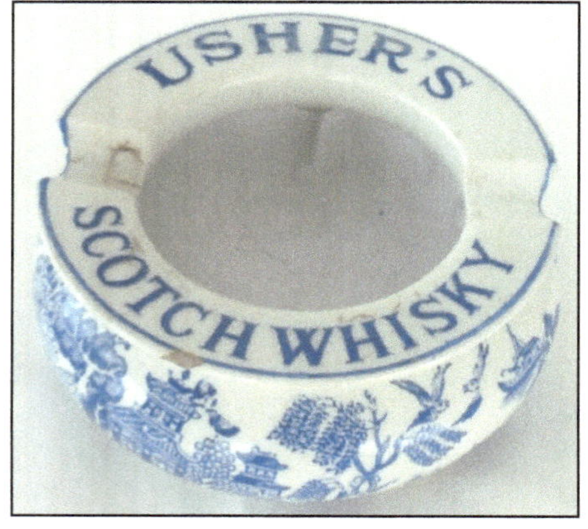

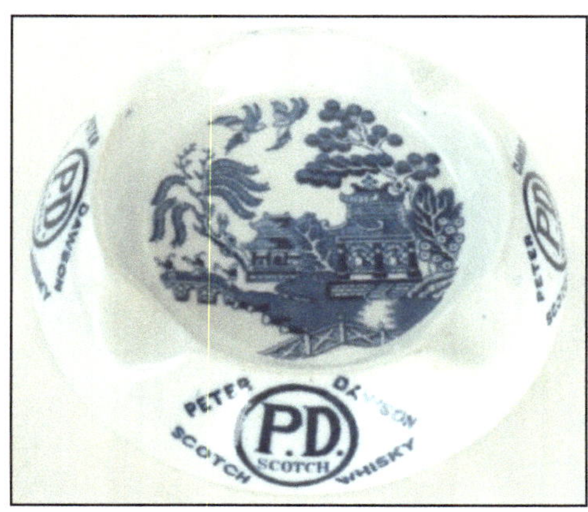

BAKING

On this page I've brought together a selection of items that can be used when baking at home. As you can see it is not diffi-cult to have a Blue Willow Pattern theme when working in the kitchen. Pictured are flour sifters, cup cake holders, a rolling pin, measuring cups, a recipe holder, recipe cards measuring spoons, an oven glove and paper plates.

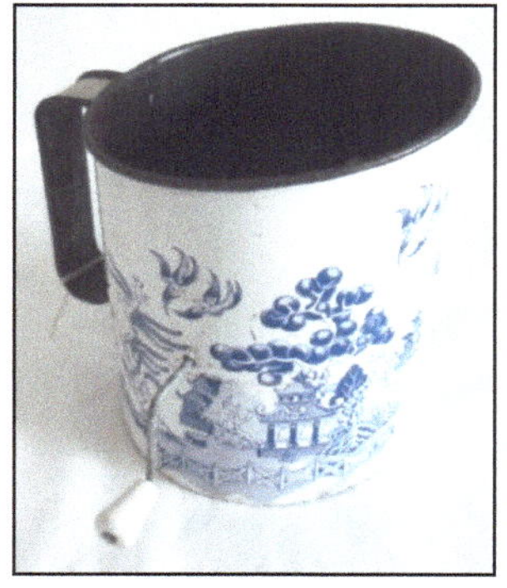

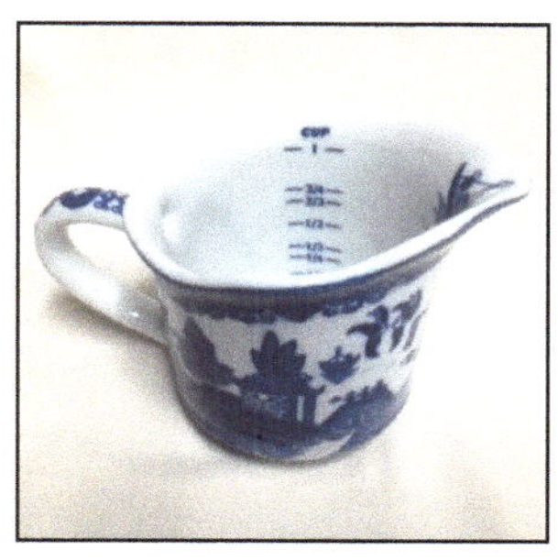

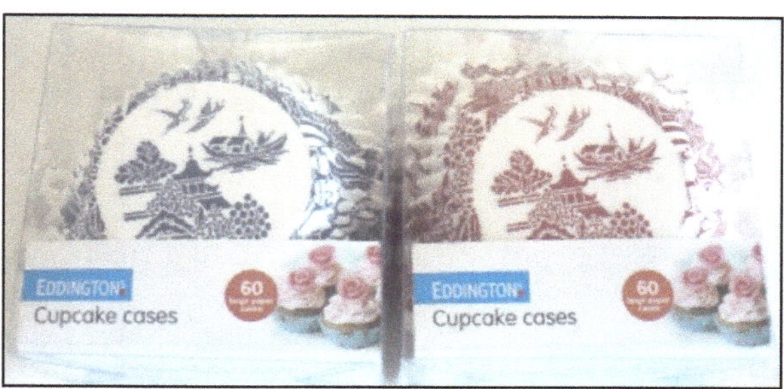

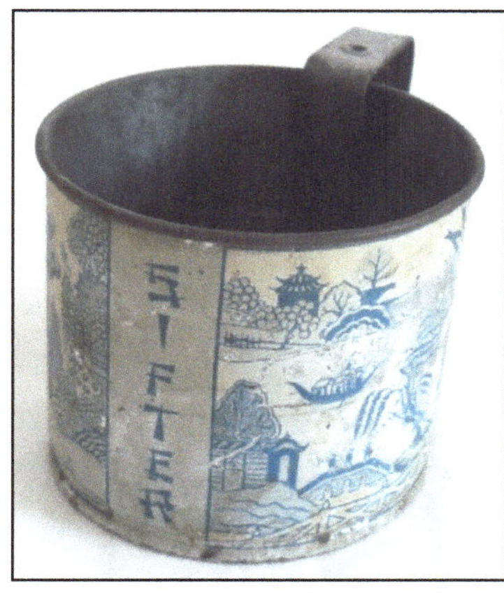

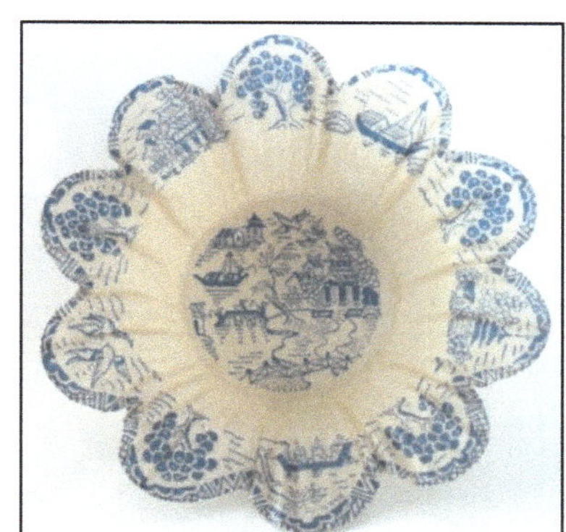

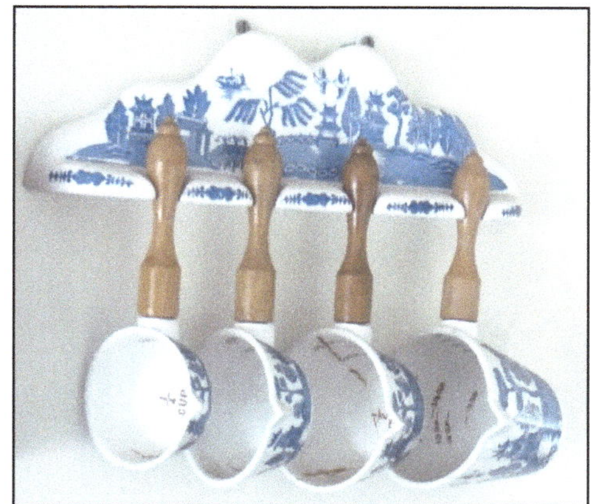

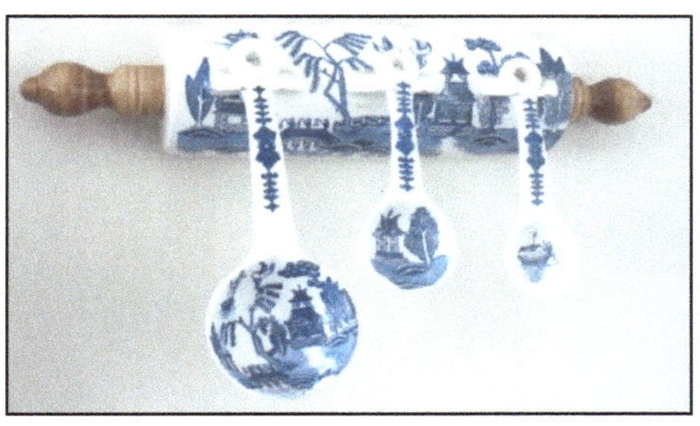

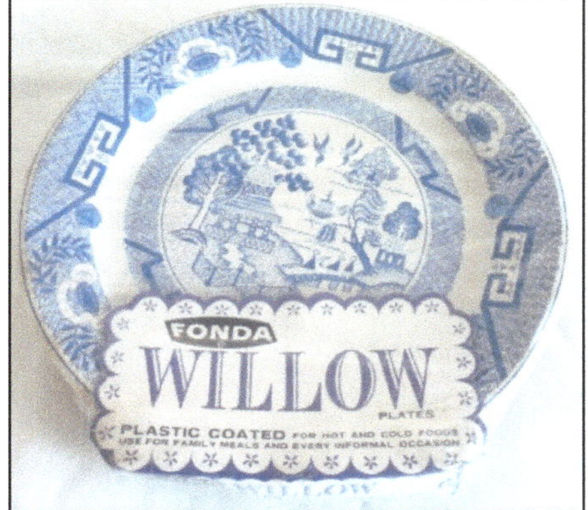

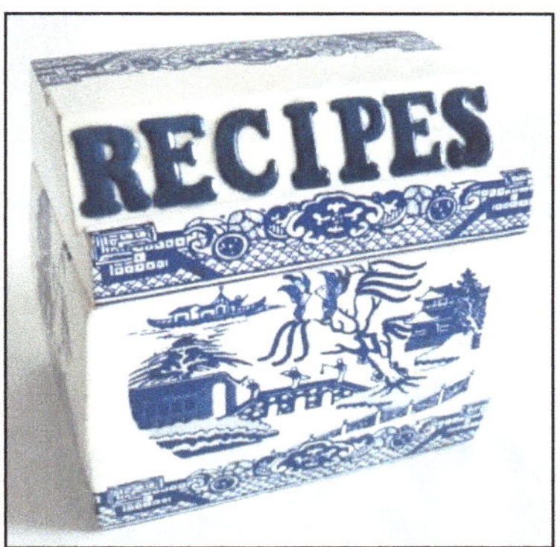

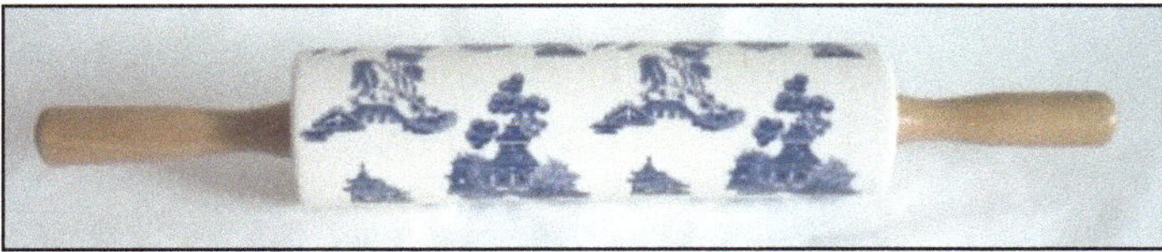

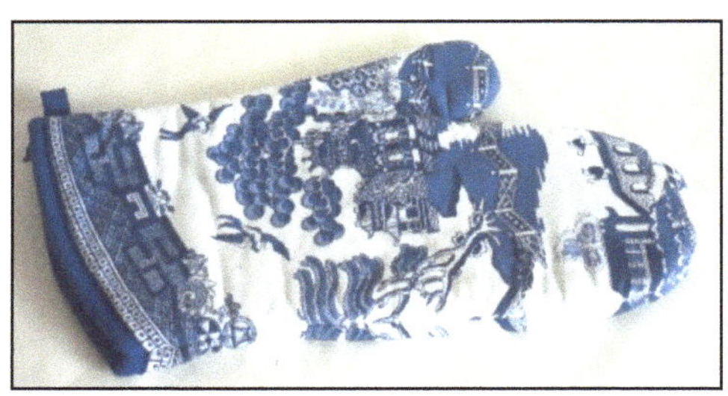

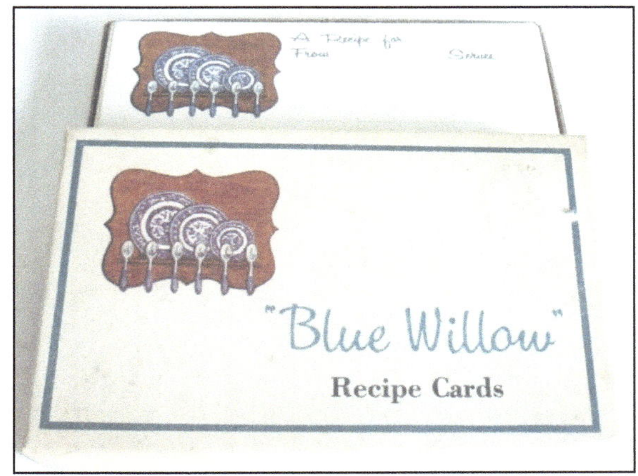

BELLS

With the first bells originating out of China around 2000 BC, it is quite fitting that in recent times bells, well at least ceramic ones have the Blue Willow Pattern on them. Pictured here are three bells, all of which provide a lovely ring tone. In keeping with the principle of making the key components of the bell with same materials, the clapper in each of these bells is also ceramic.

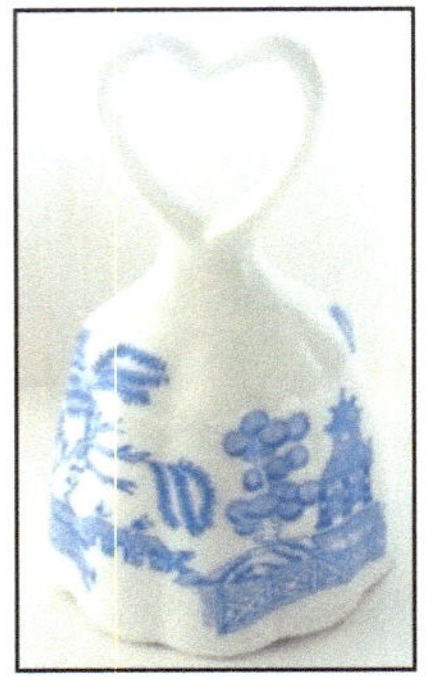 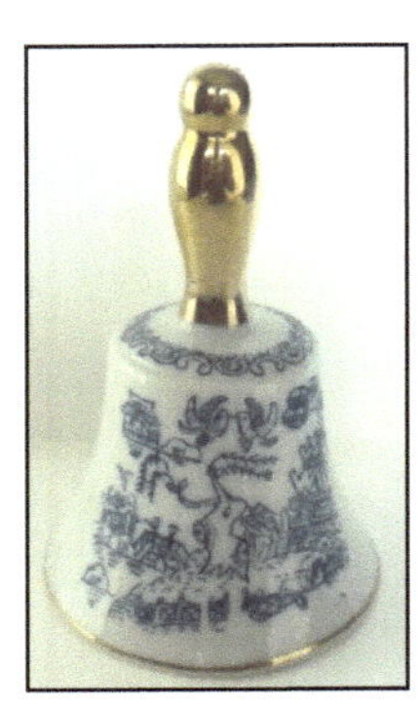 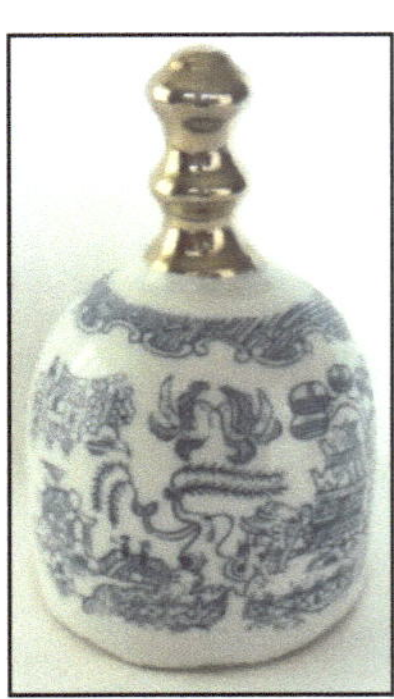

BREWERIANA

The collecting of Breweriana is almost as popular as collecting Blue Willow Pattern. Indeed with the Blue Willow Pattern featuring on numerous Breweriana items, many collectors may not realize that they are also Blue Willow Pattern collectors. The same applies to Blue Willow Pattern collectors who when they look at their collection may realize that they have a lot of Breweriana pieces. Add to that a collection of ashtrays and smoking pieces, it does not take long for a Blue Willow Pattern collector to have an interest in a lot of other collectables. On this page you'll see a sample of items showing how Breweriana and the Blue Willow Pattern come together. You'll also find some more examples in this book under Ashtrays and Smoking.

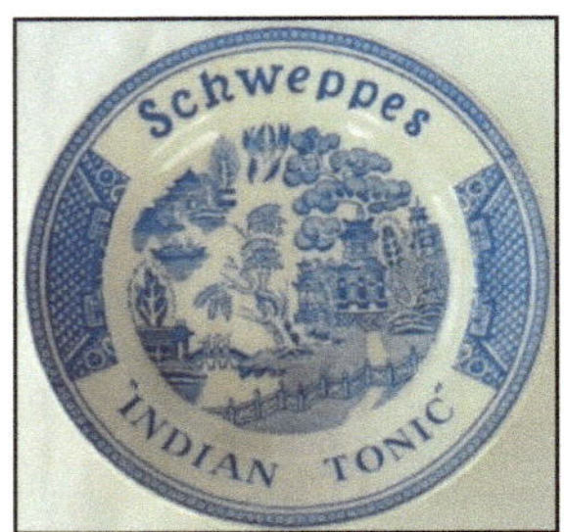

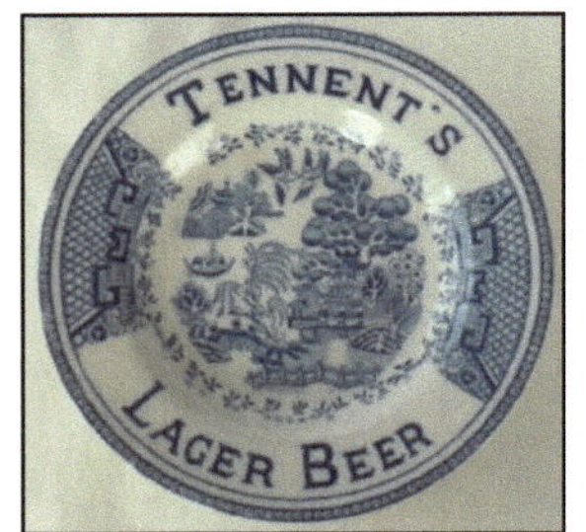

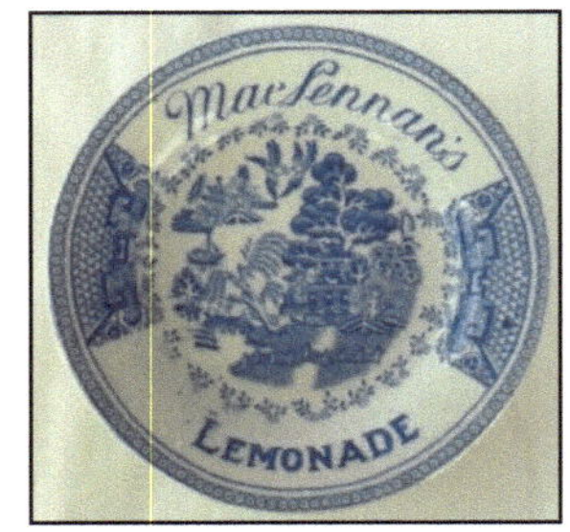

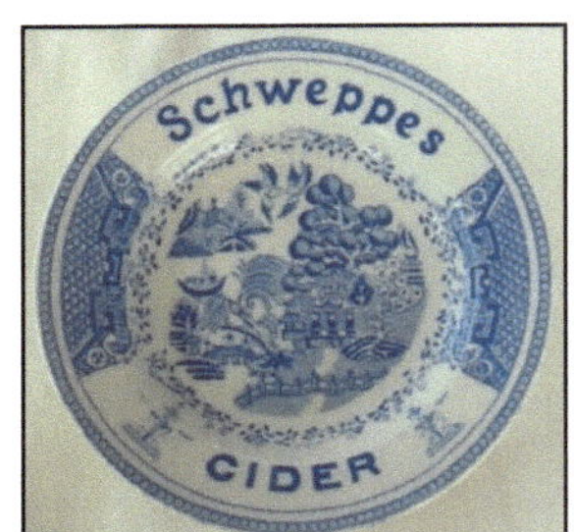

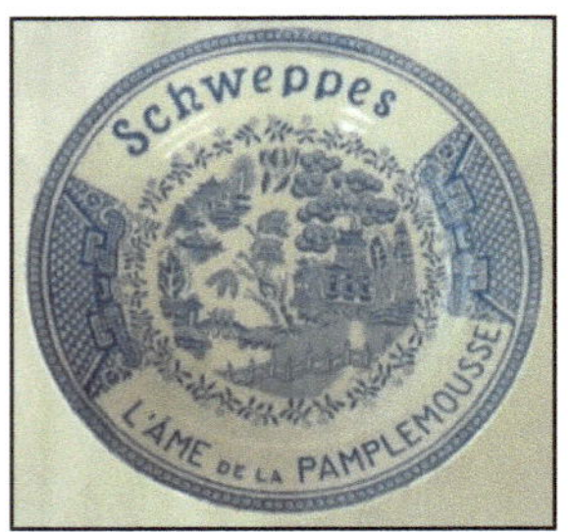

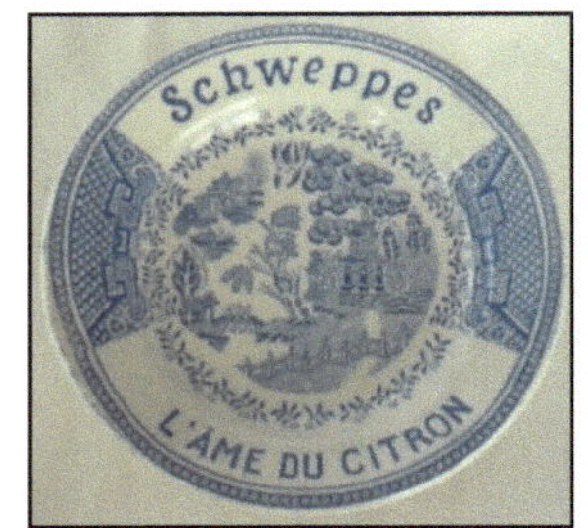

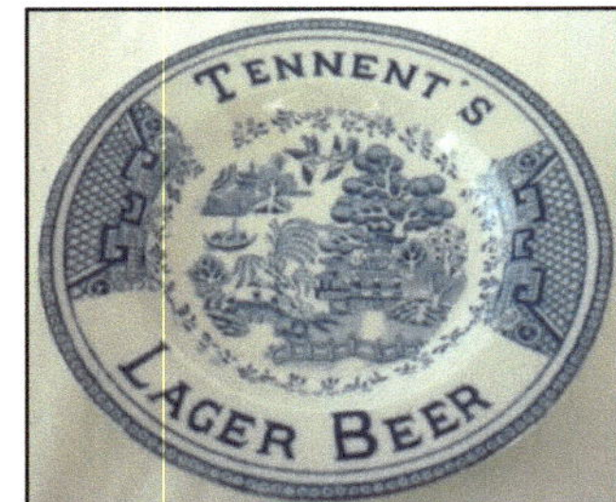

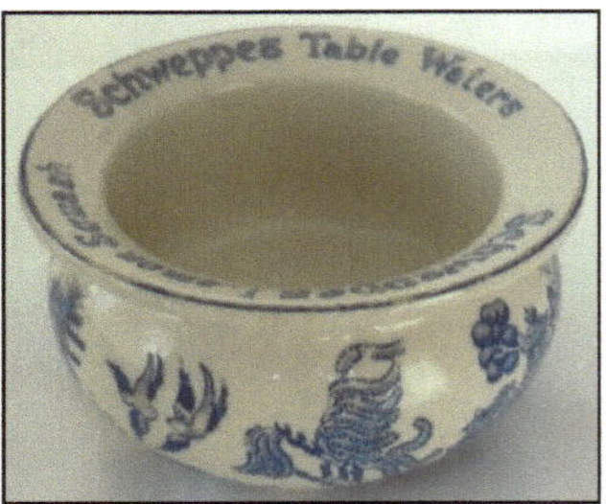

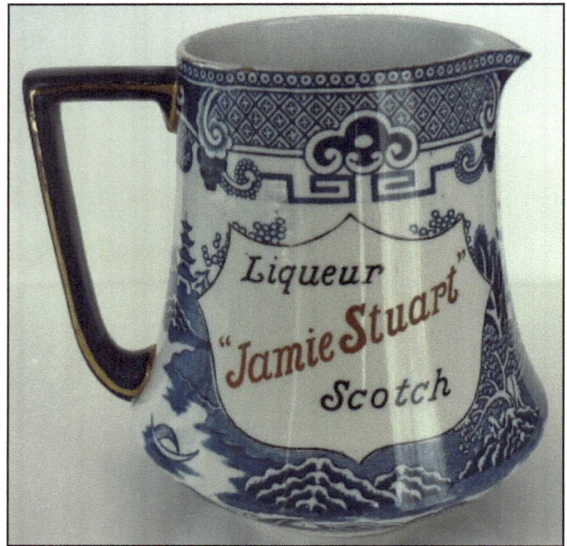

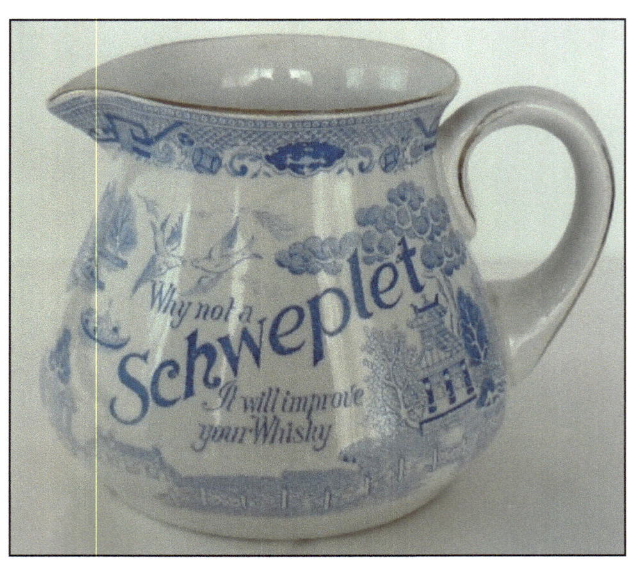

BRIGHT & MULTI COLOURED (POLYCHROME)

While it is instinctive to associate the colour blue with the Blue Willow Pattern, you'll see on the next two pages the numerous colours that have been used instead of just blue.

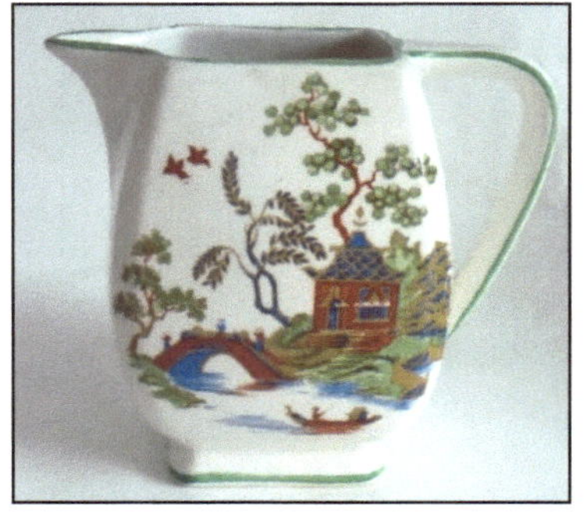
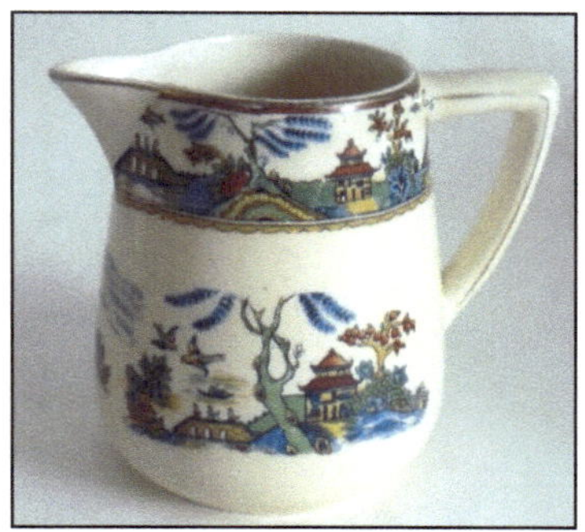
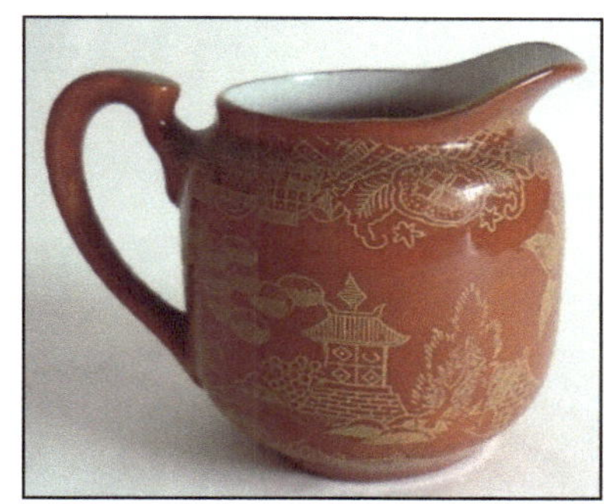

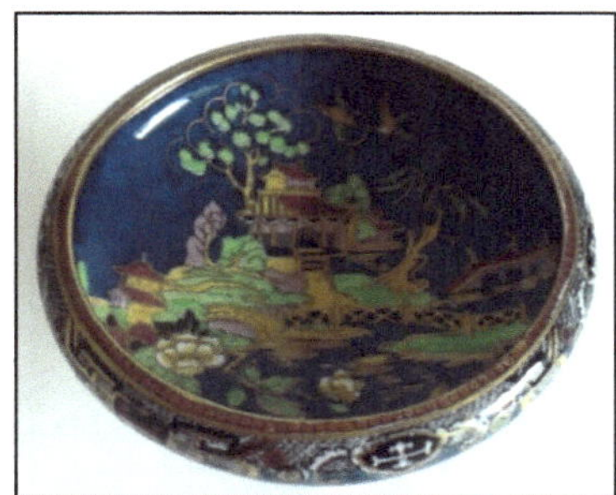
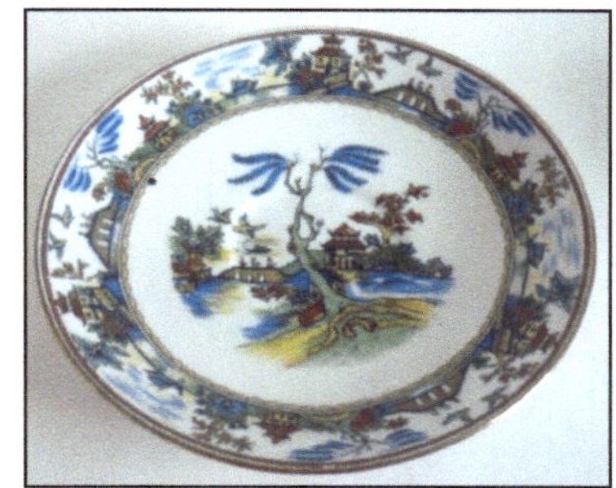
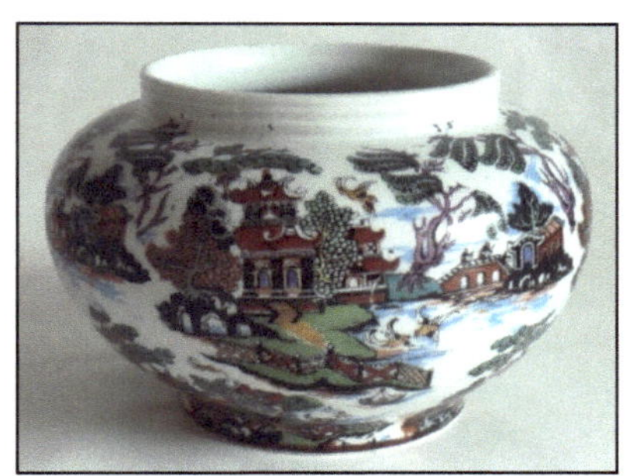

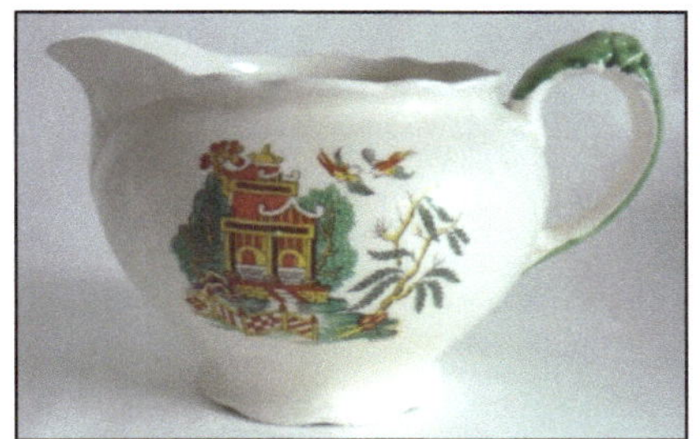
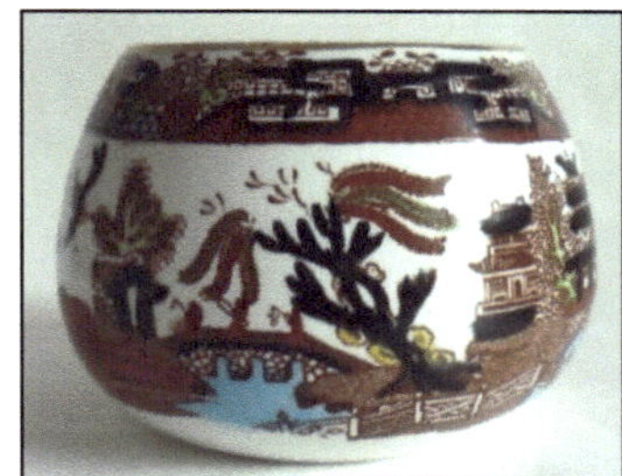
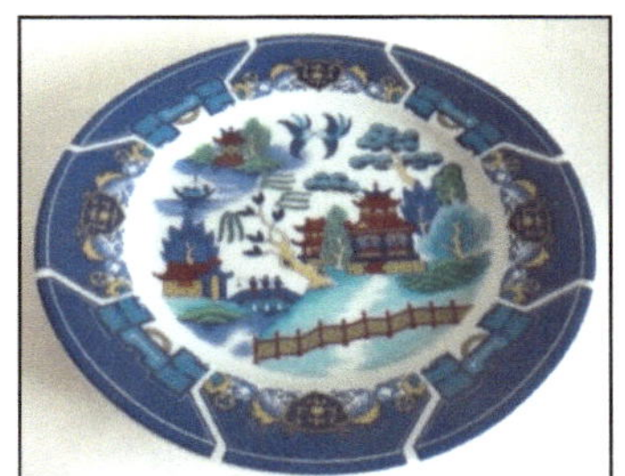

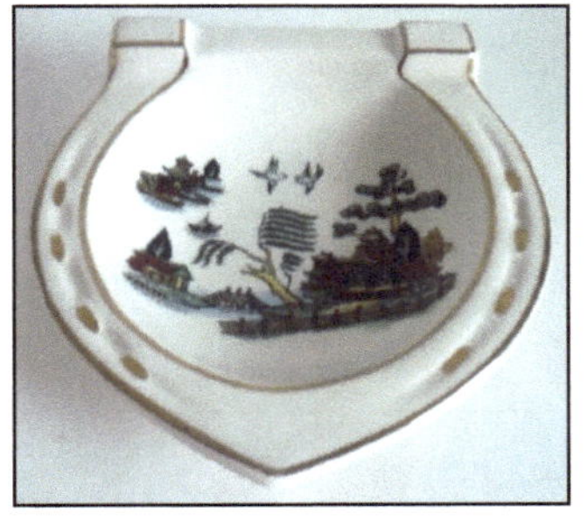
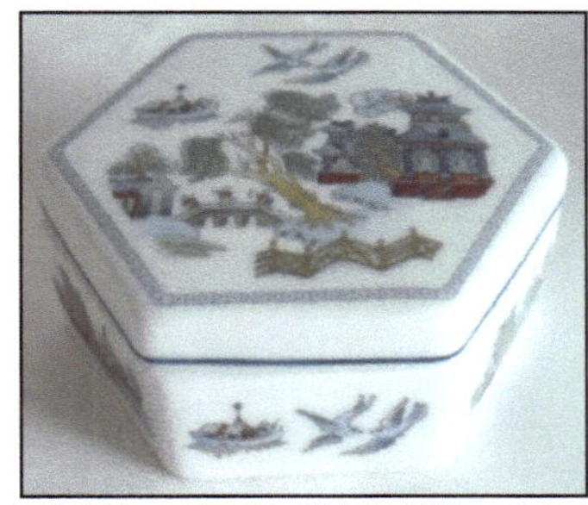
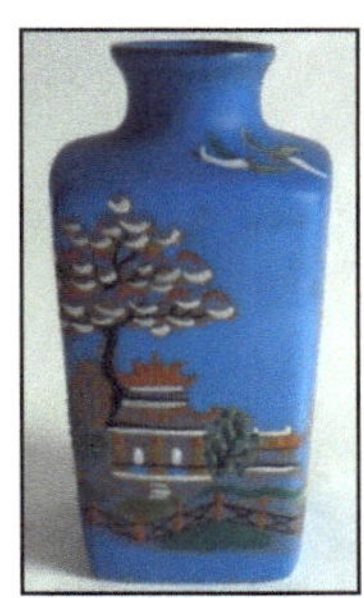
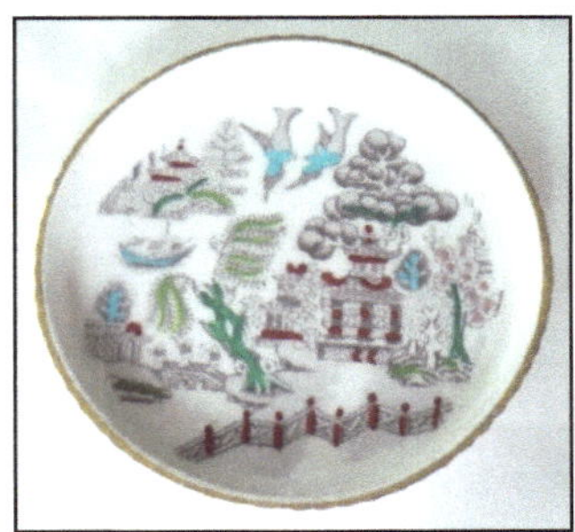

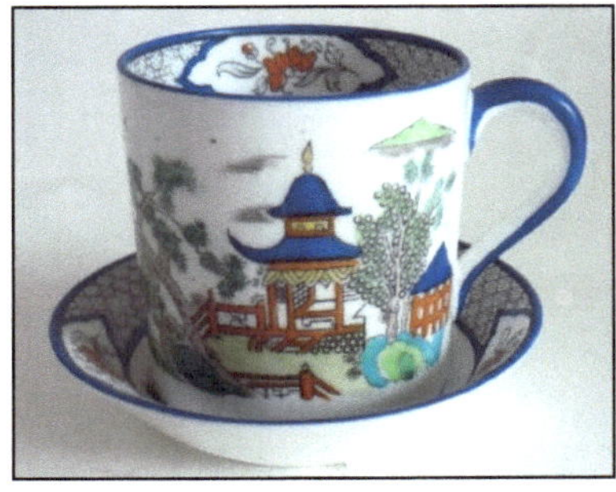
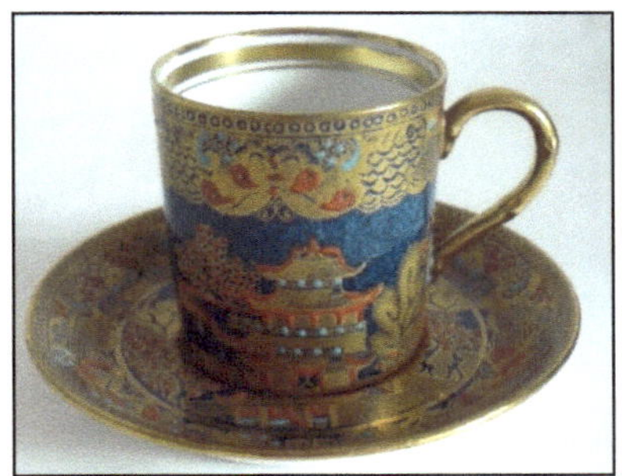
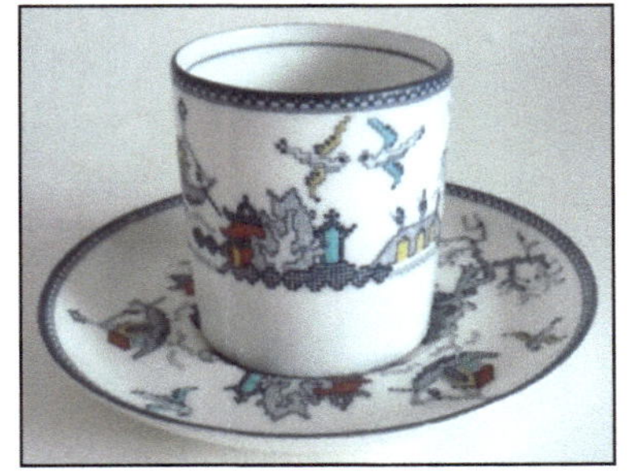

BRIGHT & MULTI COLOURED (POLYCHROME)

The many colours of the Blue Willow Pattern are continued on this page. While all of these pieces are very interesting, a particular favorite of mine is the Doulton piece pictured bottom left. This piece in green and gold is considered rare by Doulton collectors, being made between 1902 and 1922.

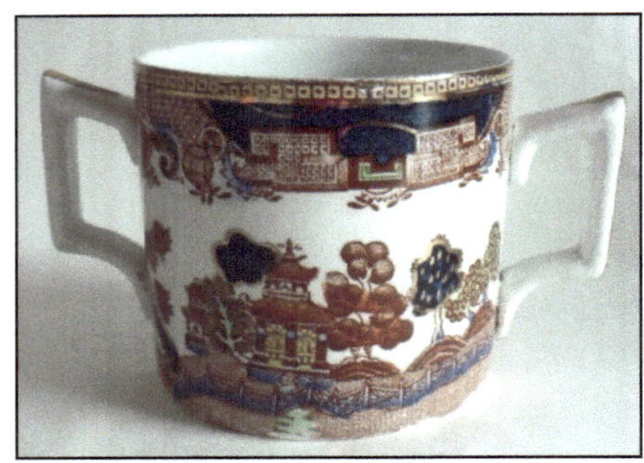
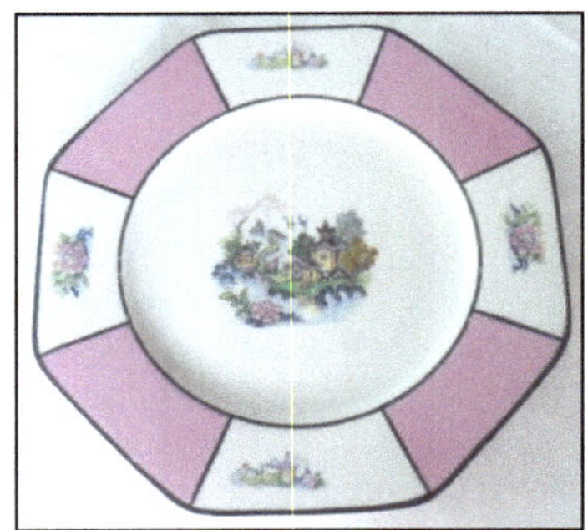
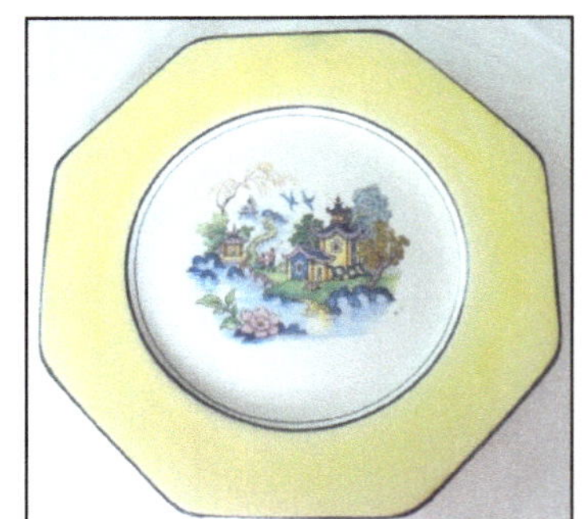

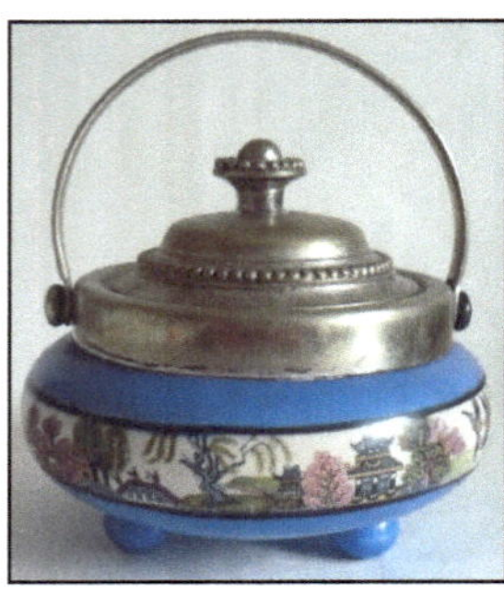
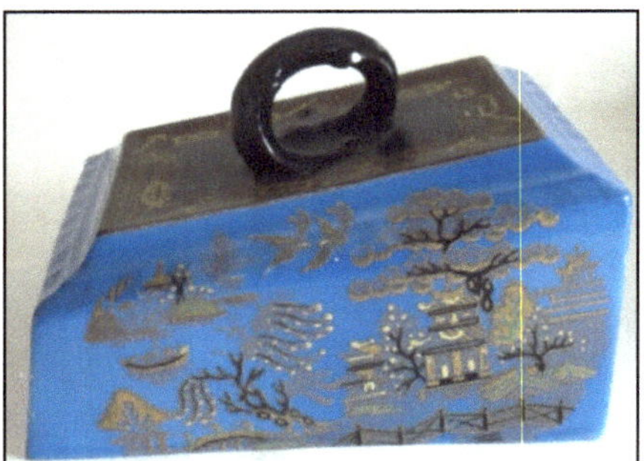
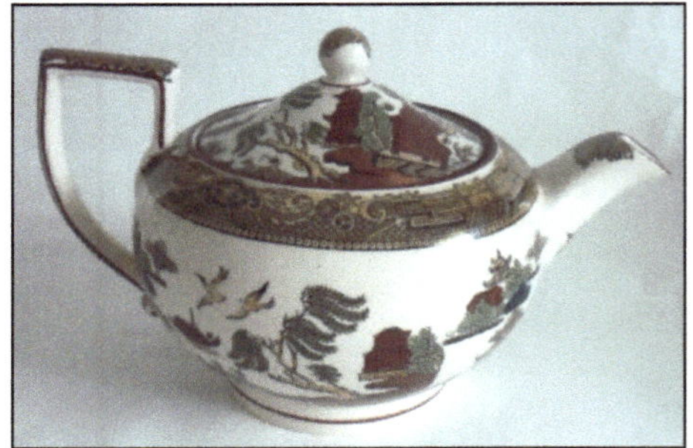

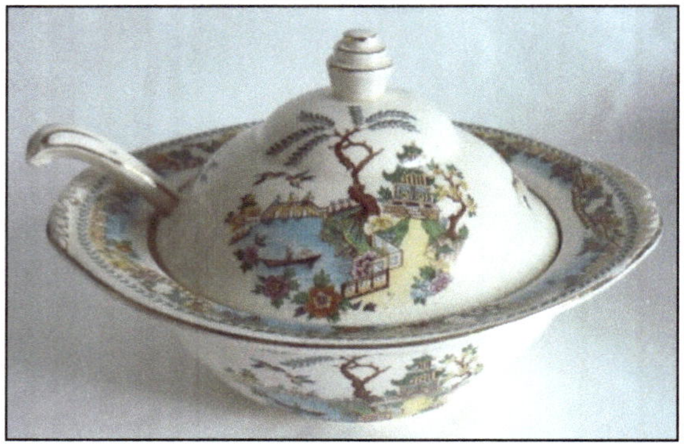
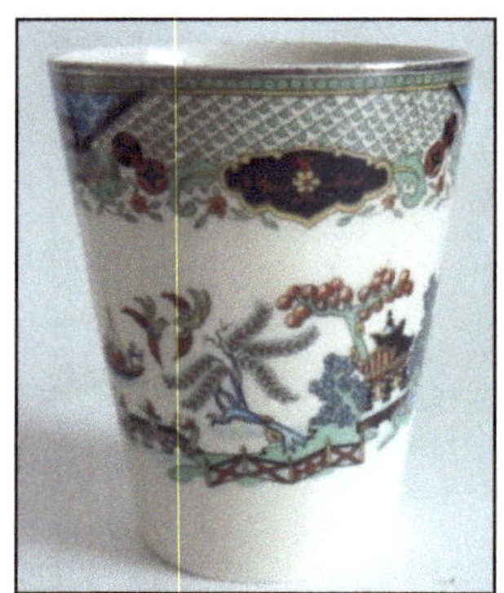
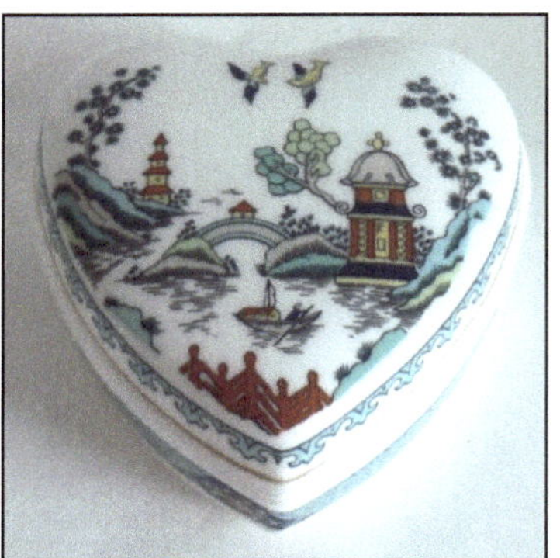

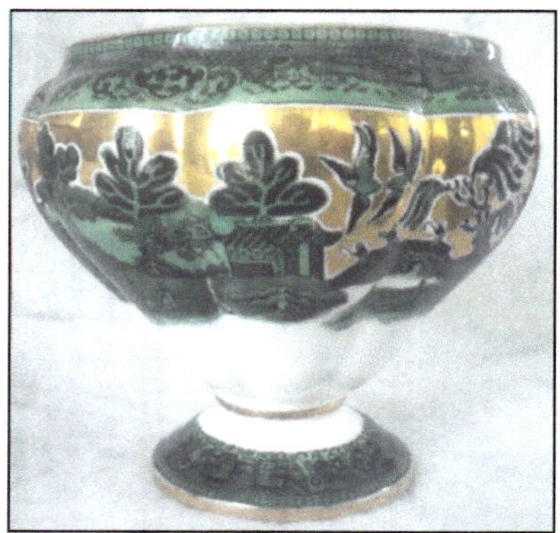
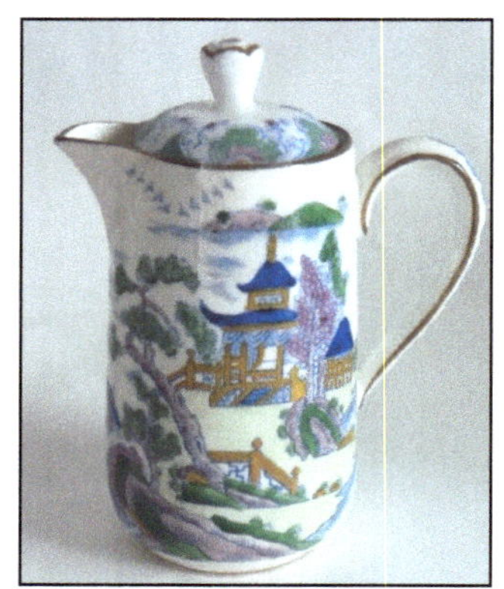
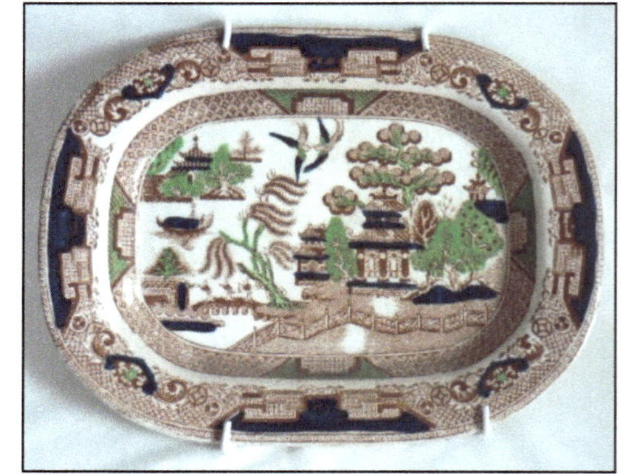

BUTTONS

To the left we have a pair of buttons made from brass, they are quite small, measuring just over an half inch in diameter. On the right are a set of four glass buttons measuring just over one inch. These are of modern day production and can be sourced on internet trade sites such as EBAY.

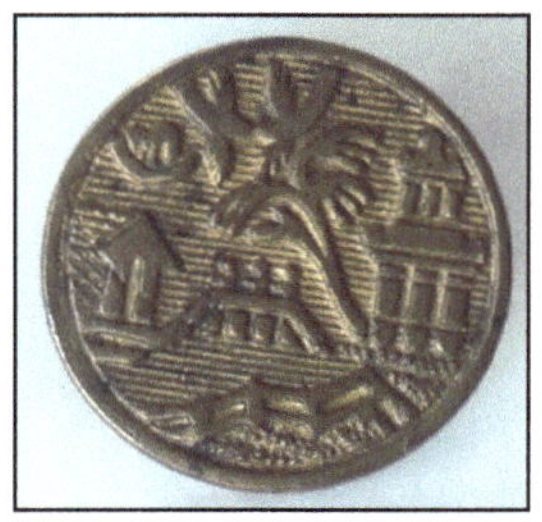 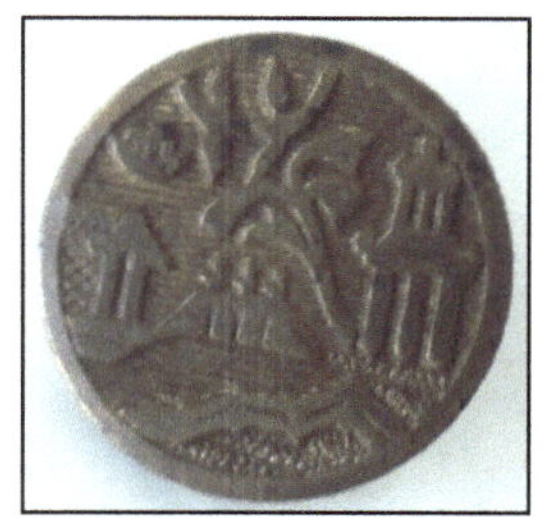 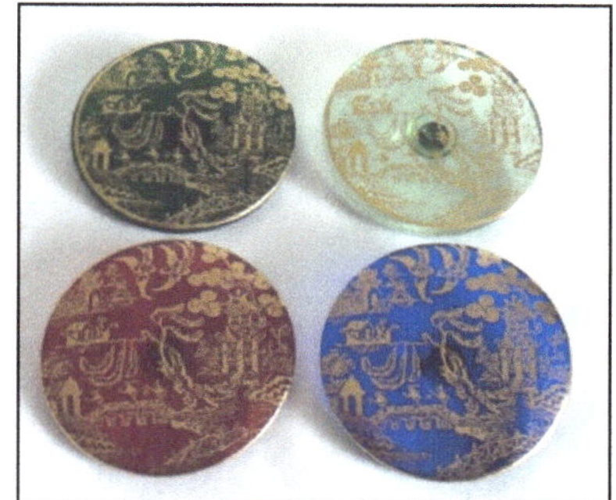

CANDLES

Wicked candles as we know them were invented by the Romans, though it was not until the 1960's that candles with the Blue Willow Pattern were seen. The candles seen here in red and blue are made in the UK by Price's. The blue set comes complete with the legend of the Blue Willow Pattern. With the Blue Willow Pattern being used since the late 1700's there is a possibility that candles using the pattern dating before the 1960's may yet be discovered. However the reality very much is that candles were a practical necessity and once used, if they did display a pattern (of any kind), well it just melted away. A collection of candles would not be complete without a snuffer. The one pictured right is made by Coalport, and while it looks great, it has not been used. There is a possibility that there are candle snuffers out there which are made of brass or other metals such as silver and have on them the Blue Willow Pattern. There are plenty of other metal objects which have the Blue Willow Pattern, so there is a good chance a metal Blue Willow Pattern candle snuffer exists, indeed pictured in this book is a metal match box holder, so let the search begin.

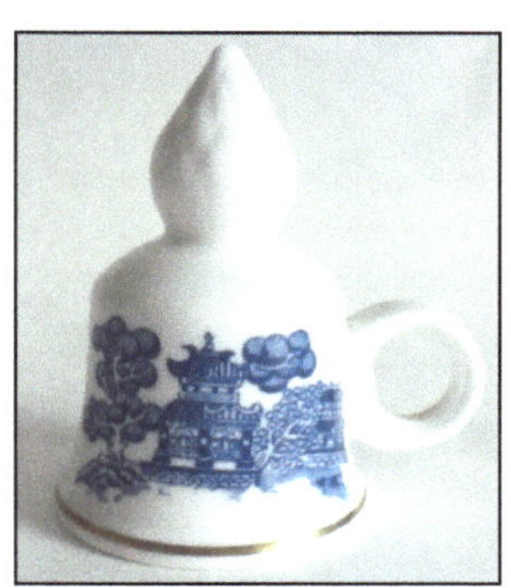

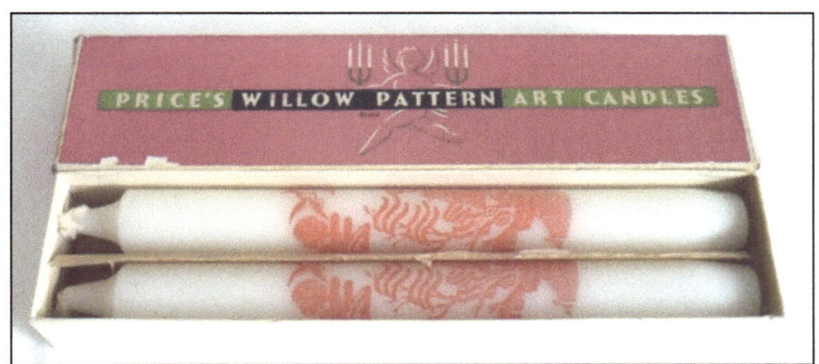

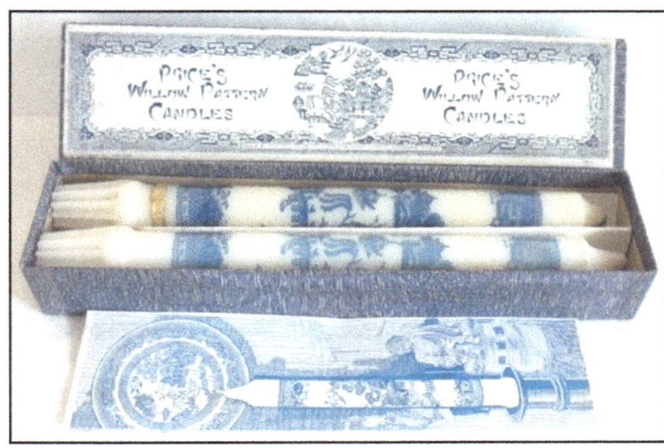

CHAMBER POTS

Chamber pots sometimes called guzunders, because historically they "go under" your bed, have over the years seen a number of Blue Willow Patterns applied to them. With the examples below, I remain convinced that none of them have been used for their intended purpose. I suspect that intending users will have thought twice about using these and gone elsewhere to relieve their needs, even the enamelware chamber pot to the left is not chipped.

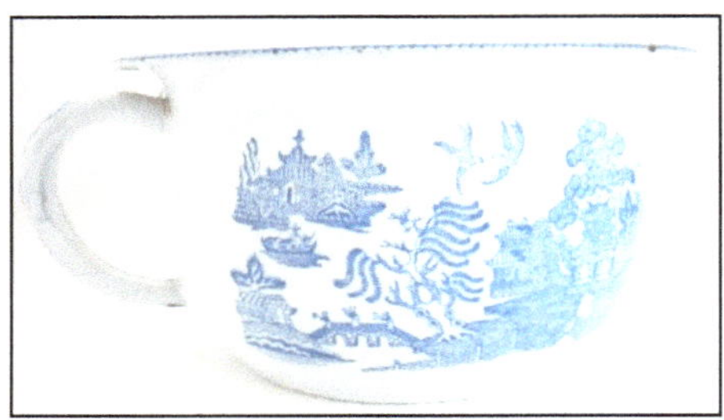 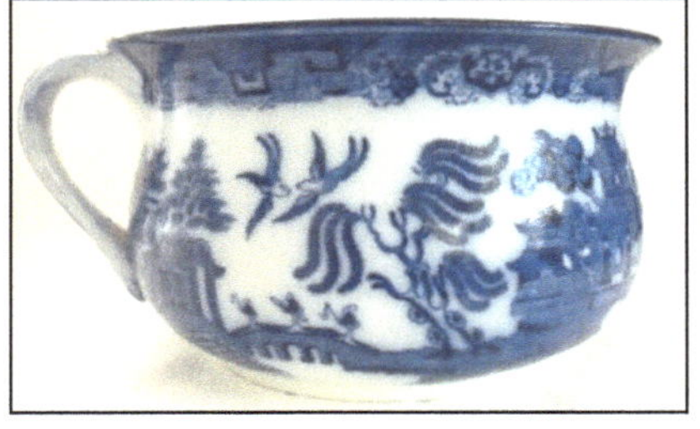 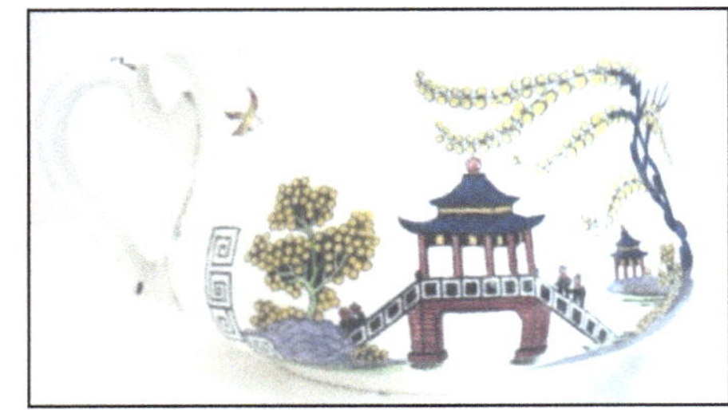

CHICKENS (AND EGGS)

The Blue Willow Pattern meets Chickens in these examples. The hen is an egg basket, the egg is a salt shaker and the plate is a small egg tray.

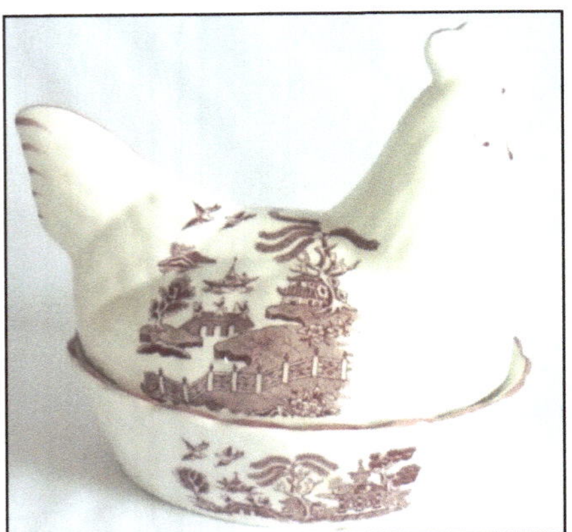 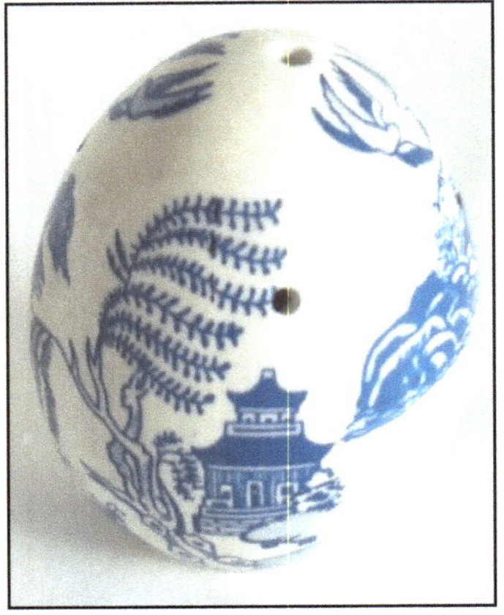 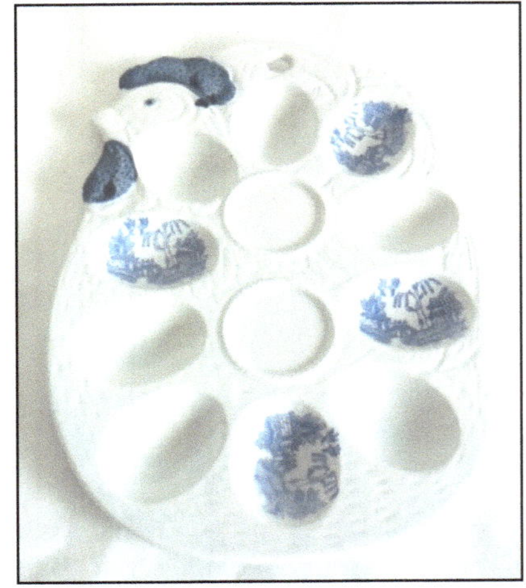

Trio of Piebirds, these are used when baking pies so that the covering pastry has a support in the centre. A chicken is featured centered and is surrounded by a duck and a goose. To the right, a boxed set of egg cups with timer.

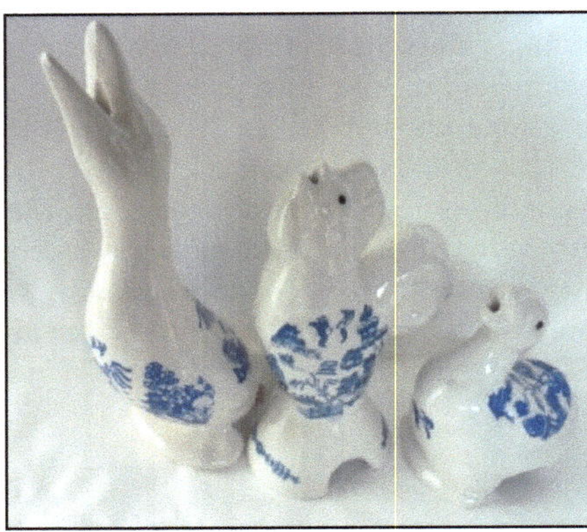 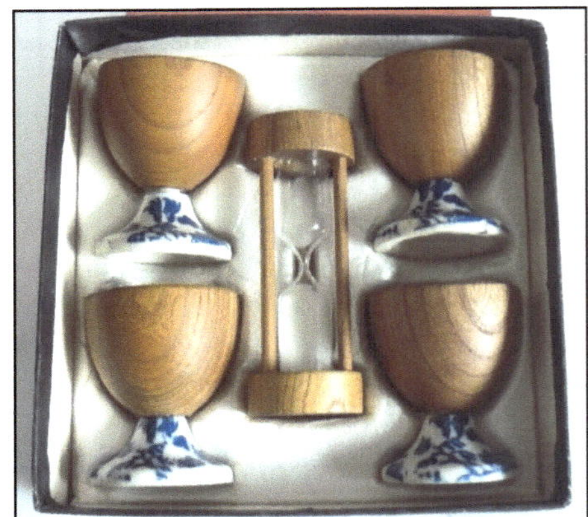

To the right, when one lifts this chicken from its basket we discover two eggs. A closer examination of these eggs reveals that that are cleverly disguised salt and pepper shakers.

Both the pieces below are dedicated to the egg of the chicken. The first is an English piece that was designed to hold four egg cups, remarkedly this piece of the set has survived, however the four egg cups are missing, perhaps like eggs, they cracked and broke. More fortunate and made of wood with a ceramic inset, is a Japanese piece which is quite resilient to being broken, though the glue holding the ceramic inset has been known to perish over time.

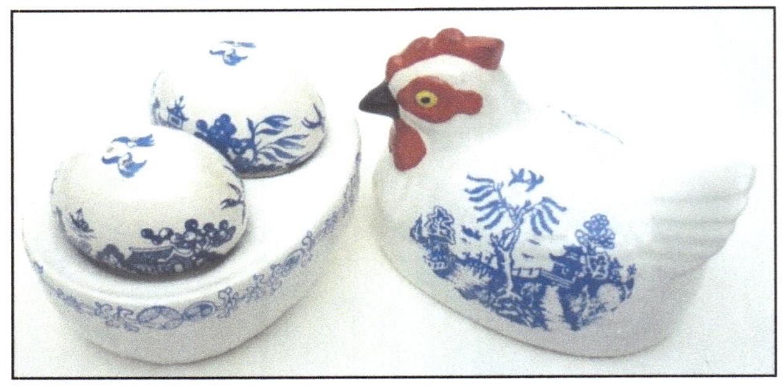

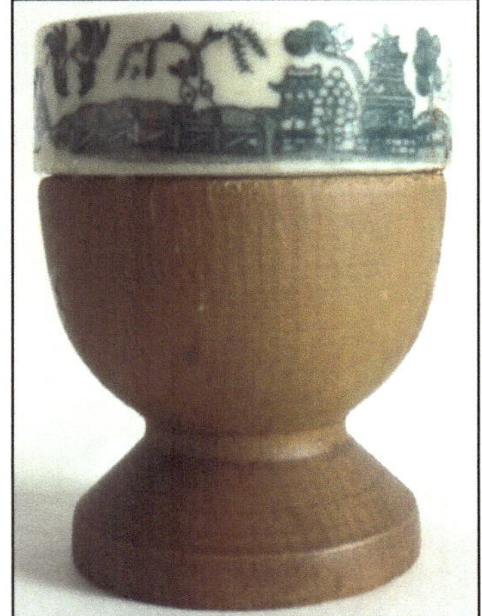 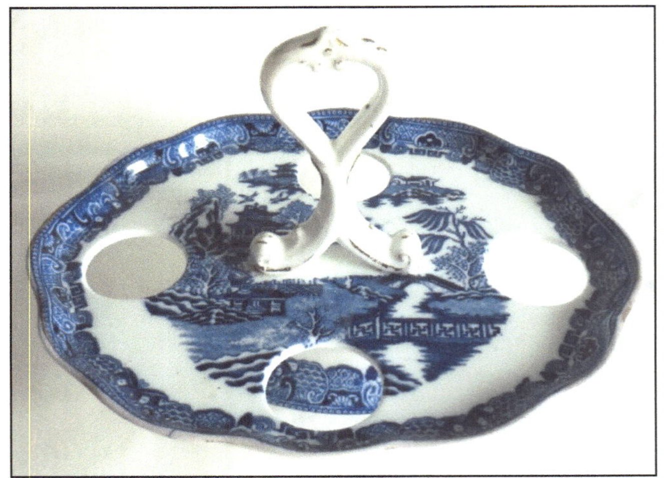

CARDS

It is quite apt that the Blue Willow Pattern has been used on playing cards. Here is a brief selection. The first known playing cards were used in China and date to the first century. While playing cards were probably used in European medieval times, it was not until 1375 when the first stories mentioning use of playing cards occurred. As we know, the creation of the Blue Willow Pattern did not occur until the late eighteenth century, so playing cards with the pattern were not seen before then. That said, one can not rule out the possibility of an early version of the pattern being used before use by English potteries.

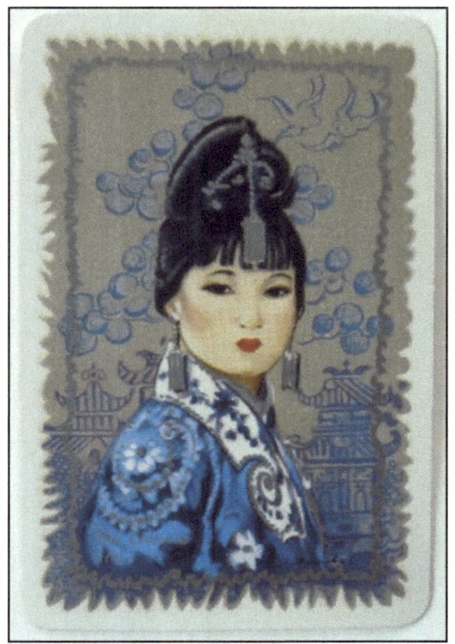
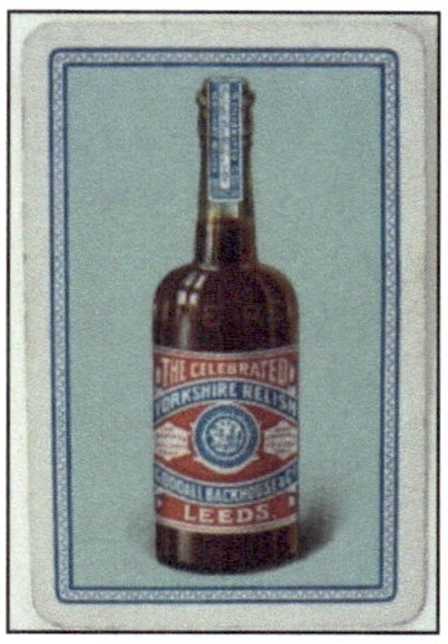
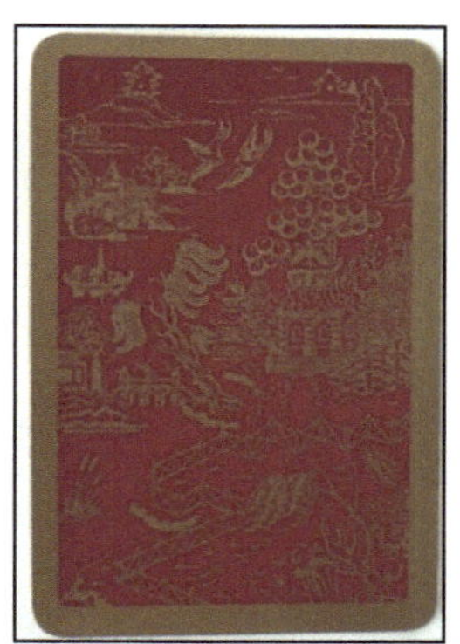
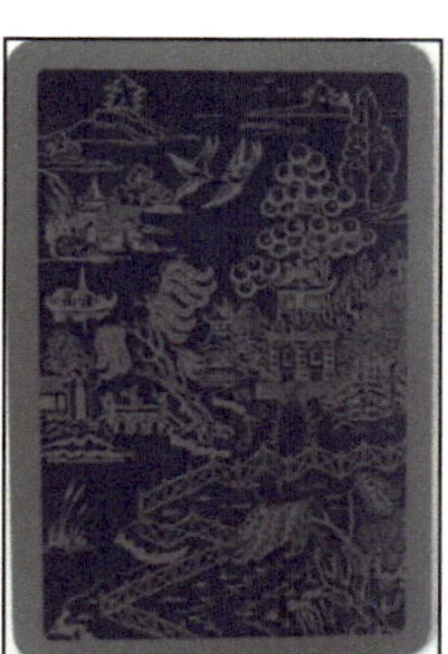
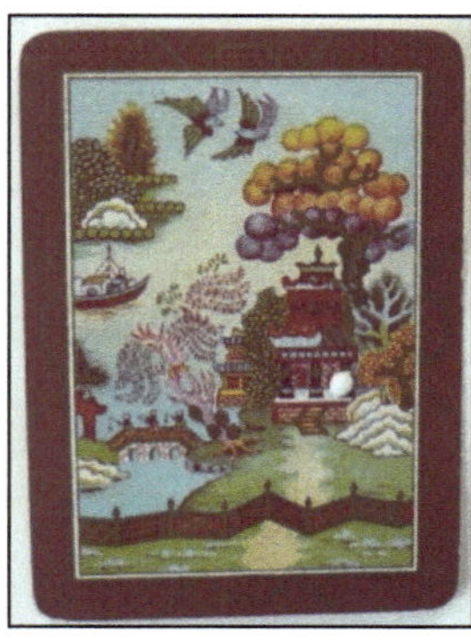
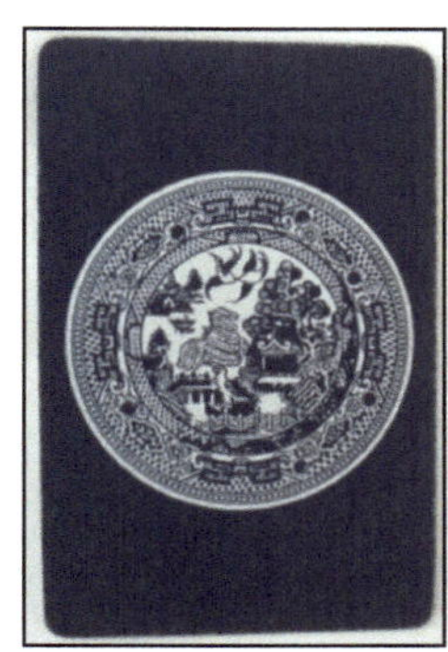
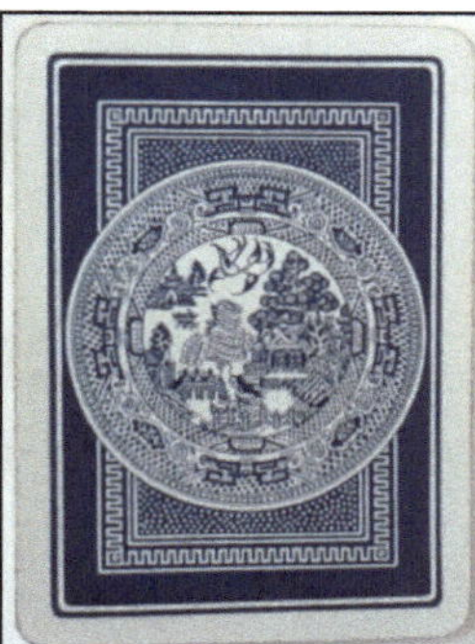

COASTERS

Coasters or placemats are probably used by every home across the country. Sometimes seen as a decoration, their use is very practical as they protect the surface from which they are laid on from the heat or cold of the item such as a plate or cup on them. Over the years their have been numerous coasters and placemats that have used the Blue Willow Pattern as a design on them. Here is a brief selection.

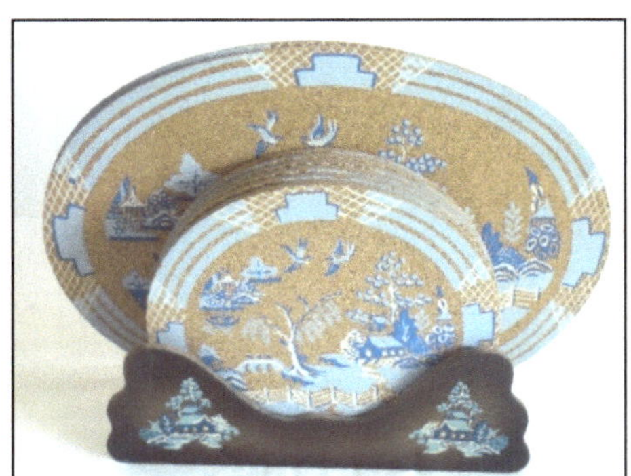
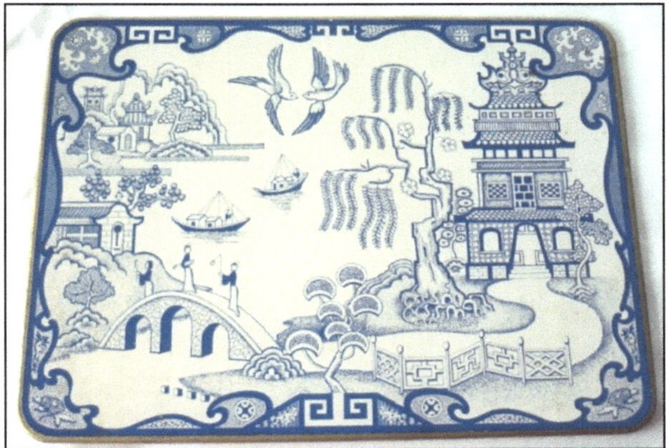
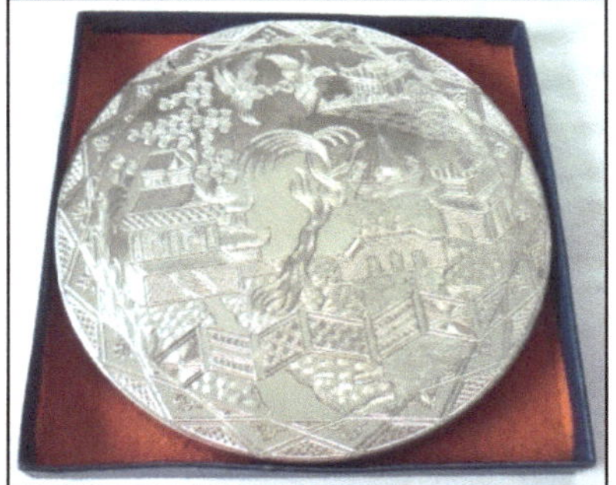
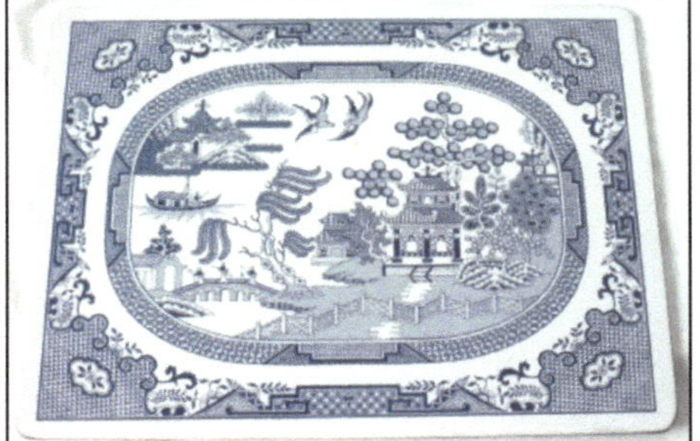
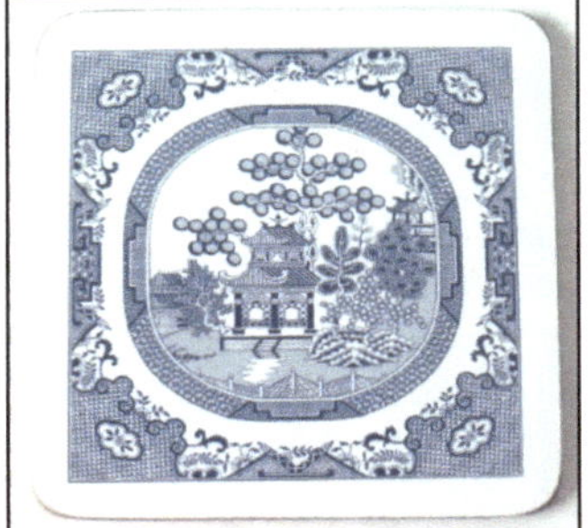

CHRISTMAS

The Blue Willow Pattern and Christmas are long time friends and can often
be seen together during the festive season. On the top row we have Christmas
decorations, the ones on the left being made by Cardew. On the next row we
have a water jug which in 1929 was a Christmas present from the Mostyn Arms,
a British pub to their patrons and suppliers. Next to the water jug is a Toby Jug
which features on a Blue Willow Pattern Christmas Card.

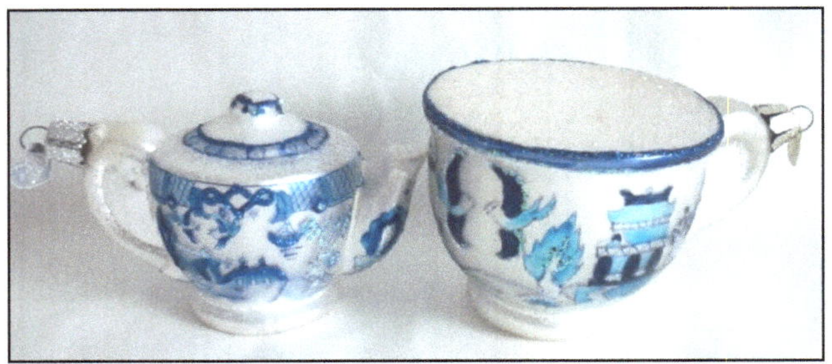

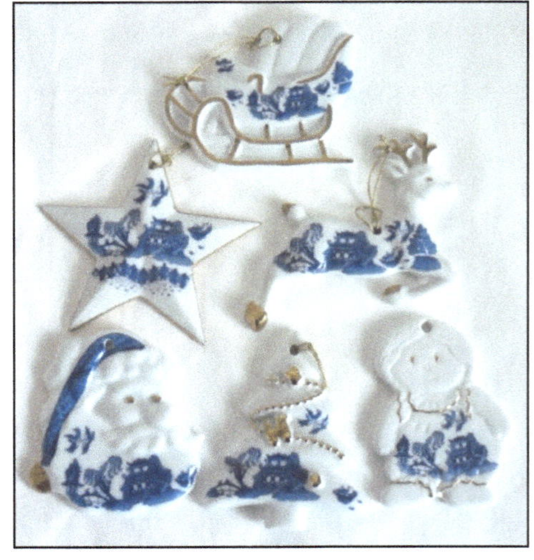

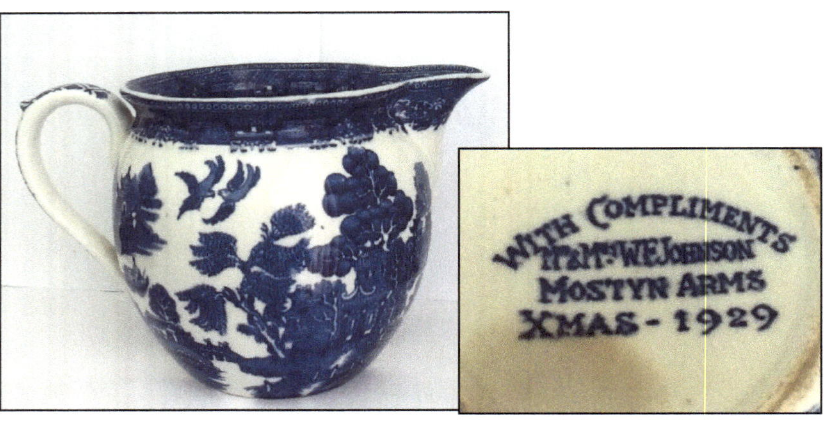

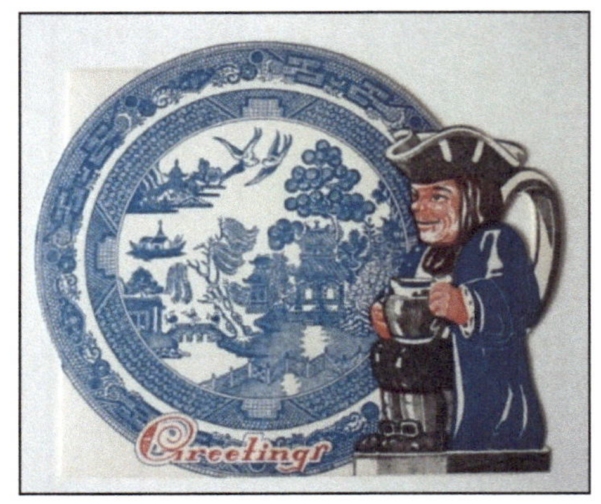

CLEANING

Whether it be washing your clothes with
one of the range of cleaning products
from *Sweet Sheets* or just washing your
hands with a cake of soap, then there is
no escaping the Blue Willow Pattern.

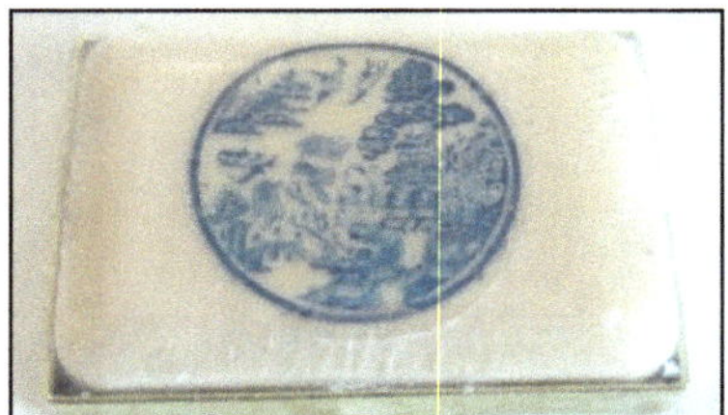

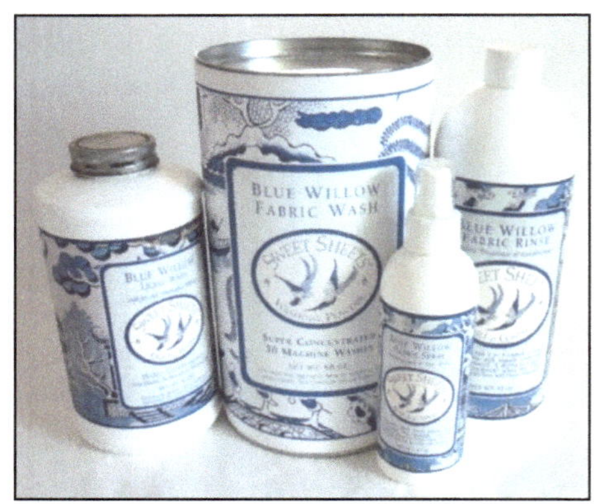

DECANTERS

Pictured left a small decanter measuring
8 inches in height with working tap to
dispense Sherry (or whatever you choose
to put in it). Centre is a blue glass decanter emboldened with the Blue Willow
Pattern in gold. To the right is a cocktail
shaker (which could be used as a decanter) which is clear glass and has the
traditional Blue Willow Pattern.

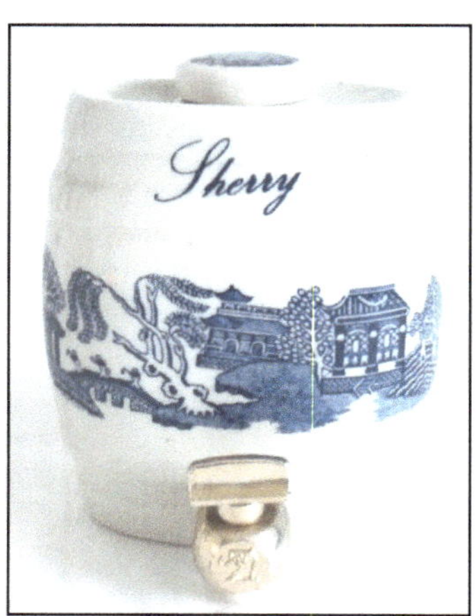

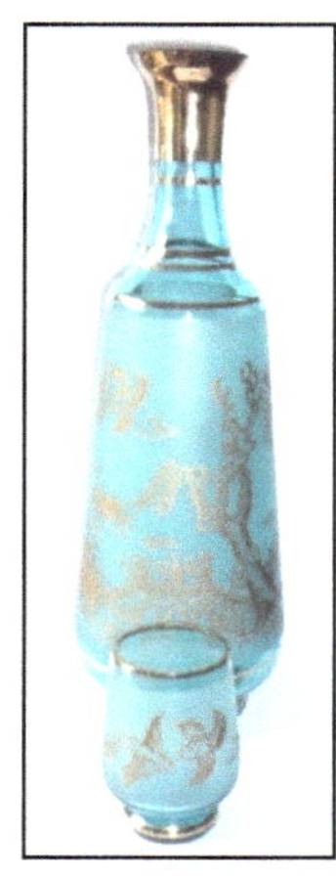

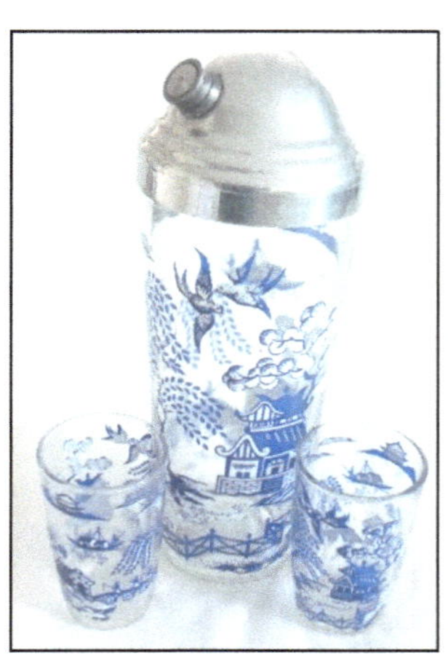

DOGS & CATS

Use of the Blue Willow Pattern is well represented when it comes to cats, less so with dogs. Though with the latter we have the popular Snack Hound which has on it the Blue Willow Pattern. With the Snack Hound, being made of several parts, the pattern goes together like a jig saw. Most of the cat items are ornamental, the top two cat items to the right have a practical use as a money box and a plant pot. As for dog representation, I'm sure there are a few more dogs out there waiting to be discovered.

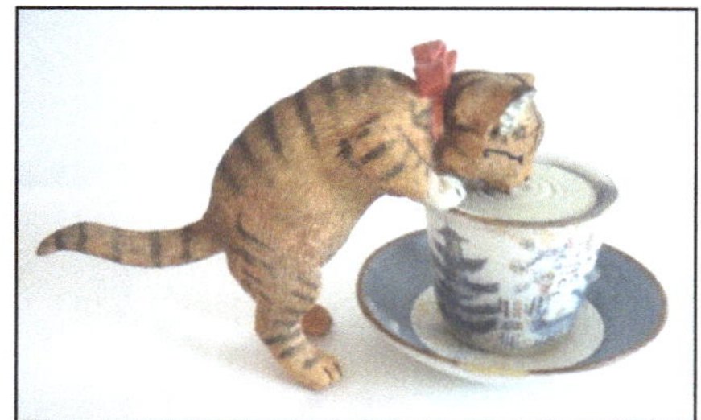
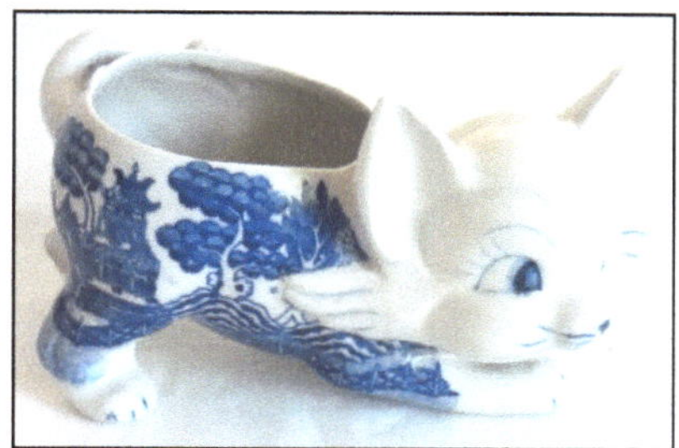
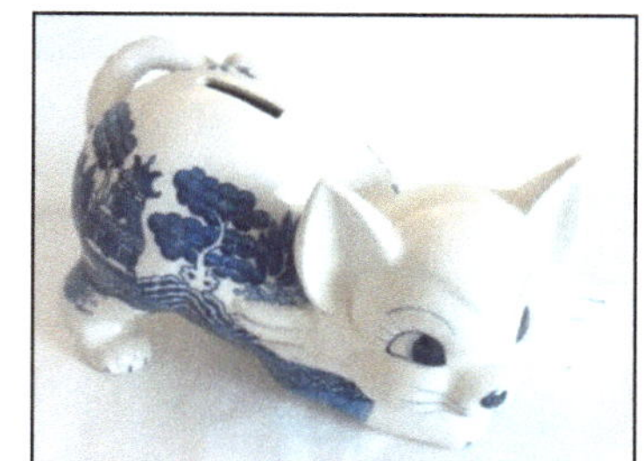
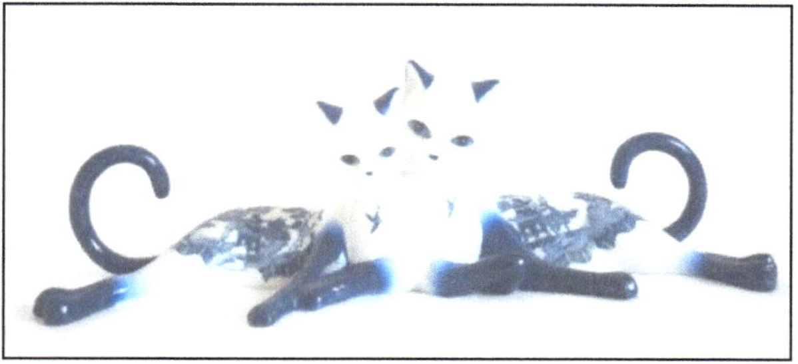
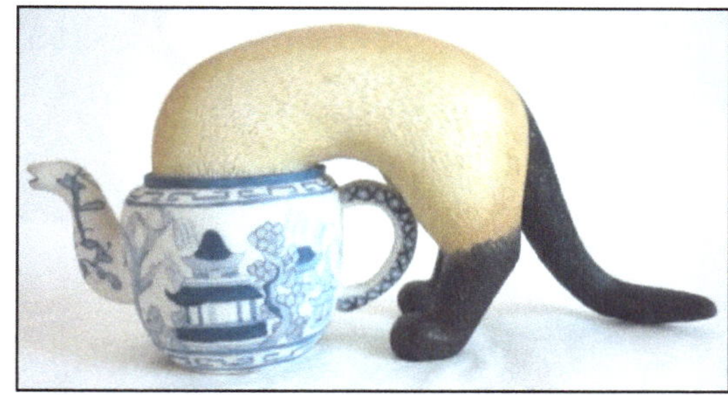
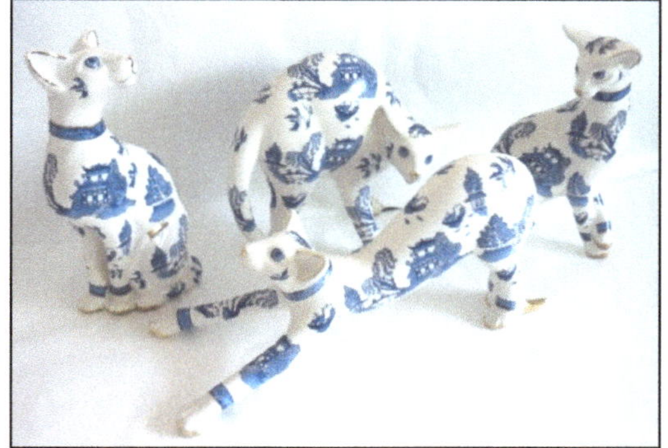
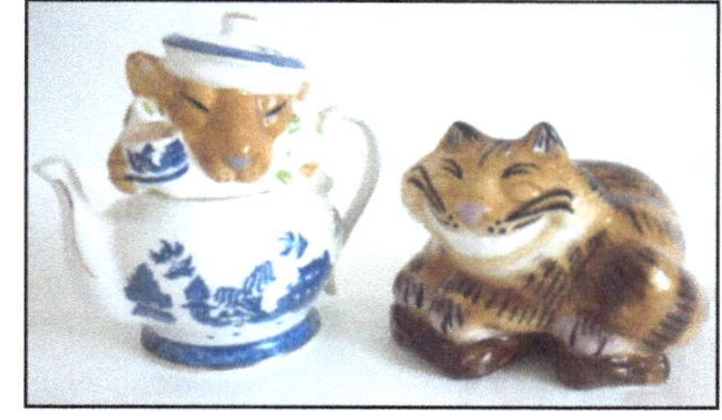
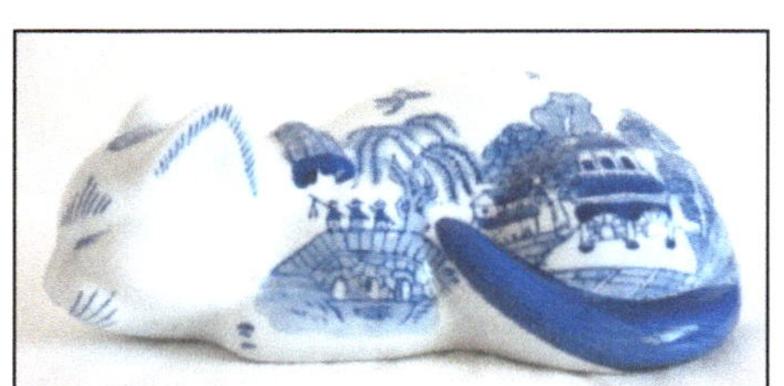
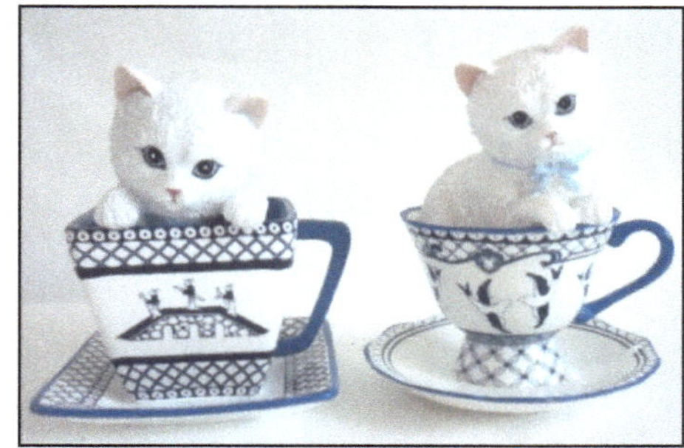
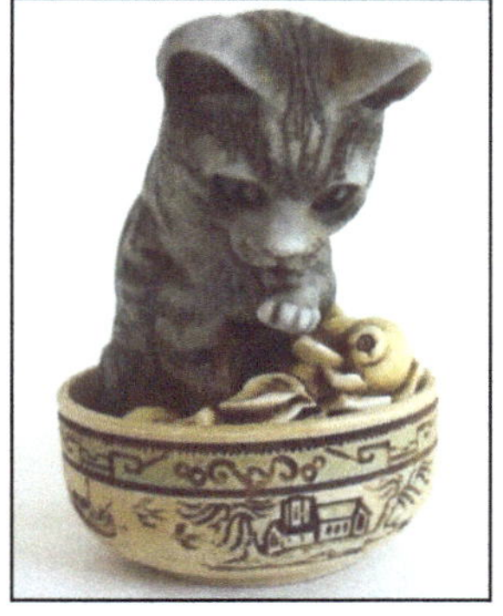
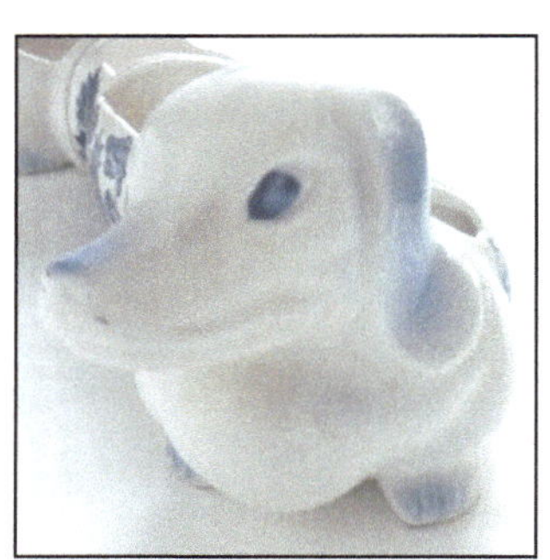
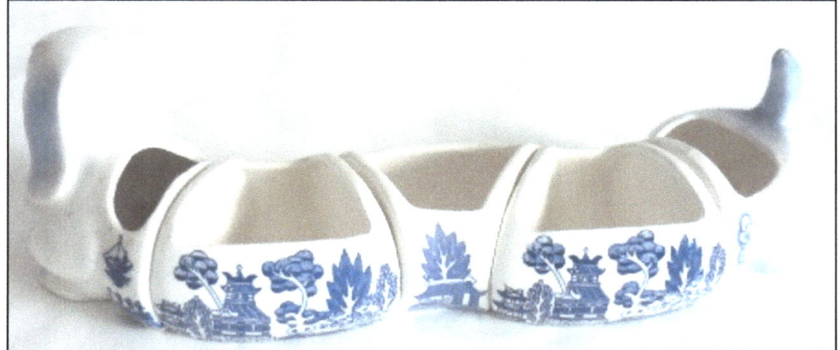

ELECTRICAL

Here we have a selection of items where the Blue Willow Pattern has been used. On the top row is a toaster in blue, this has been produced in other colours. Next to it is a tureen which has a basic warming element contained within the base of it. On the middle row is a modern day nightlight, centre to it is an enamel kettle. Next is a telephone which was made for the British market in the 1990's . On the bottom row is a lamp where the base has the Blue Willow Pattern on it.

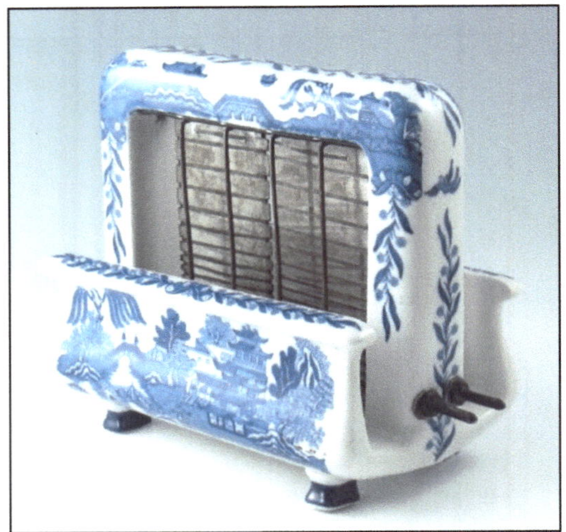
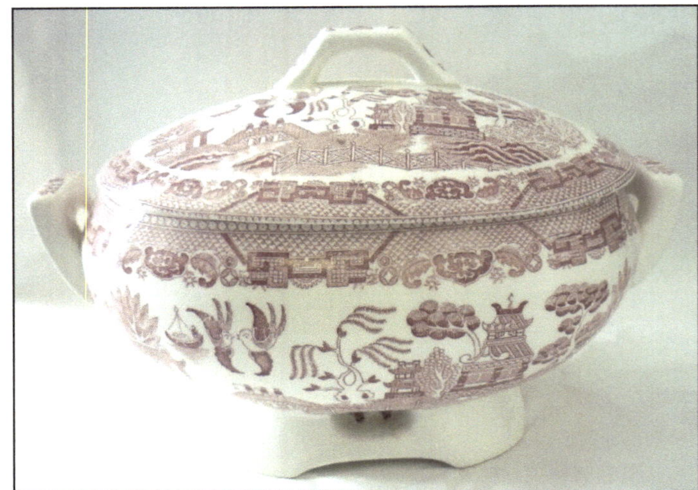

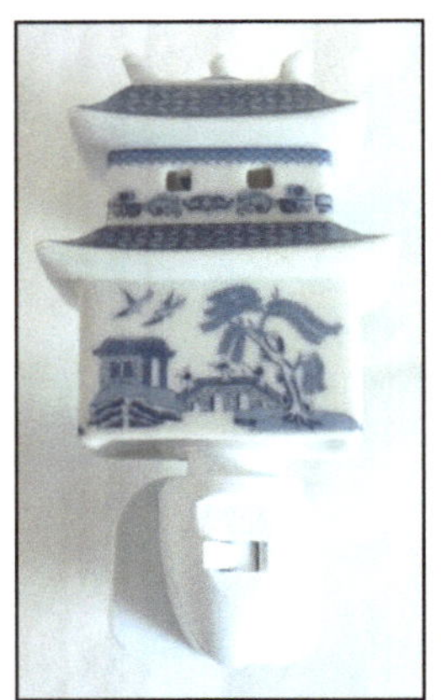
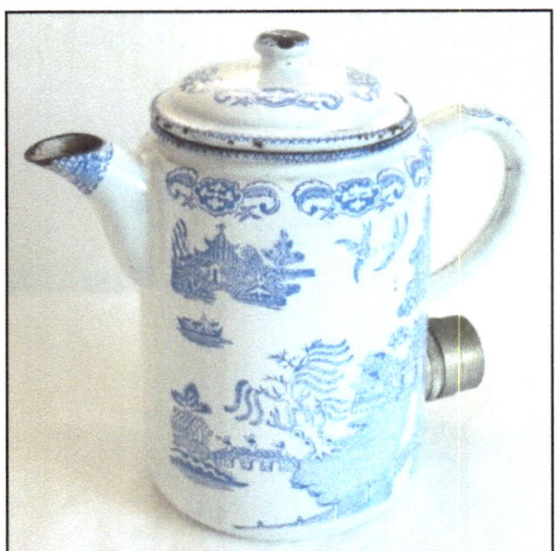
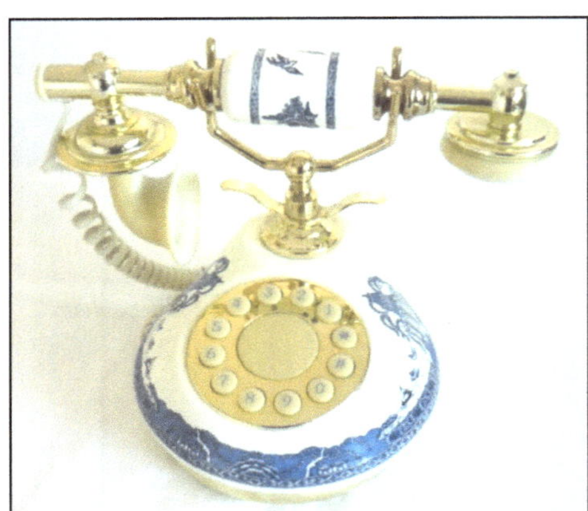

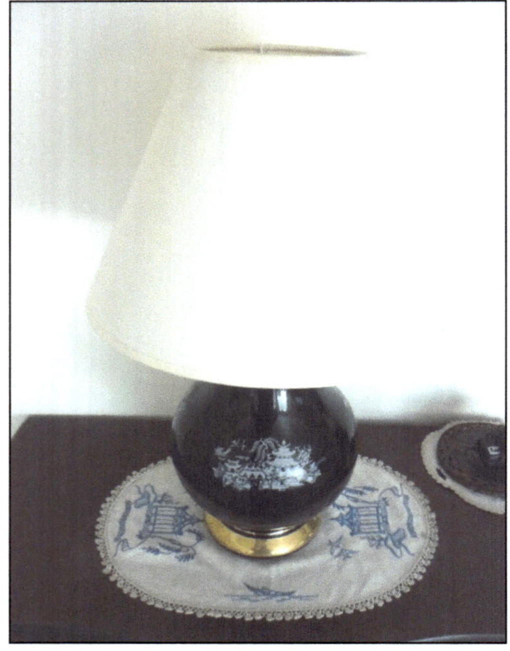
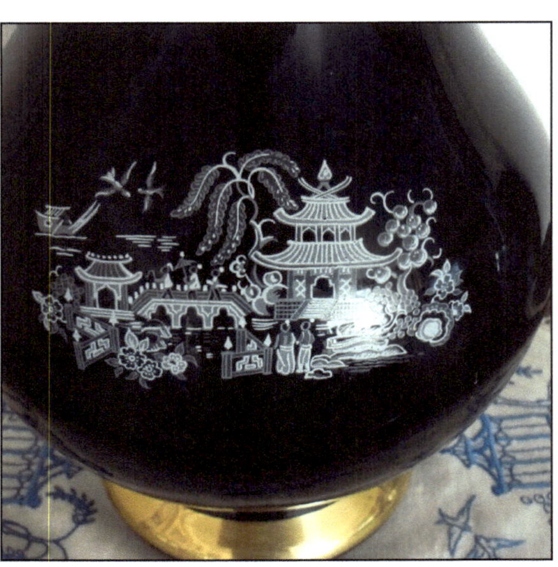

ENAMELWARE

Enamelware was the first mass produced American kitchenware which started in the 1870's and is still produced today. The process of producing enamelware pieces starts with the item being made from thin sheets of metal, it is then coated with enamel which is fused to the metal in a very hot oven. The practical use of enamel gives a clean smooth surface which can be cleaned easily. In other sections of this book examples of enamelware can be found such as an electric kettle and enamelware pots and pans. While all these items have a practical use, they also provide a good background for the Blue Willow Pattern to be used.

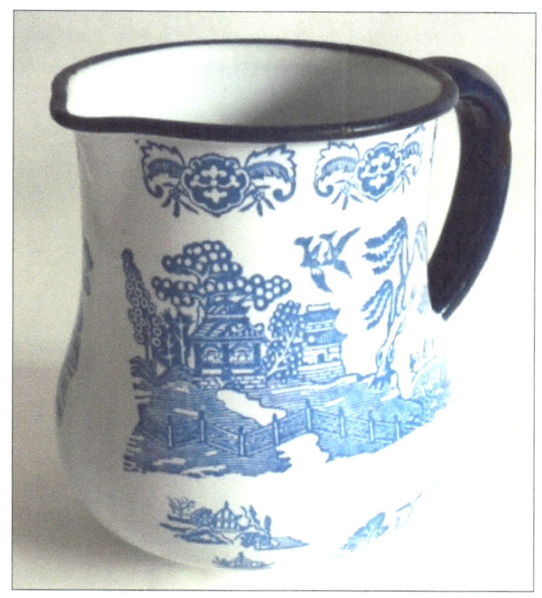

FISH

Pictured left a selection of novelty ashtrays made in Japan,, whilst appearing as fish, they could in fact be whales. To the right a small trefoil snack plate which as a centre piece has a small fish. Below is a platter which features a lobster.

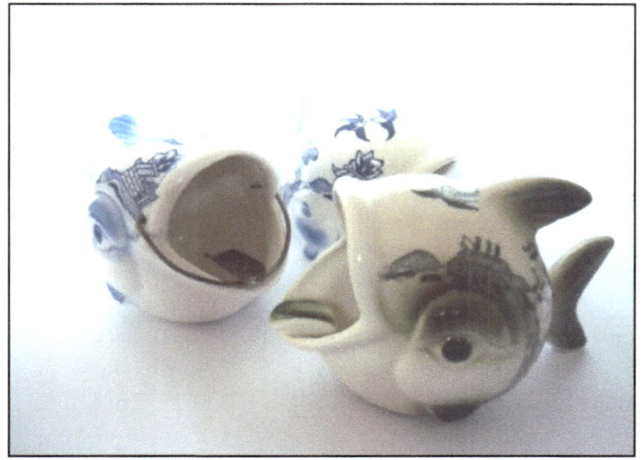

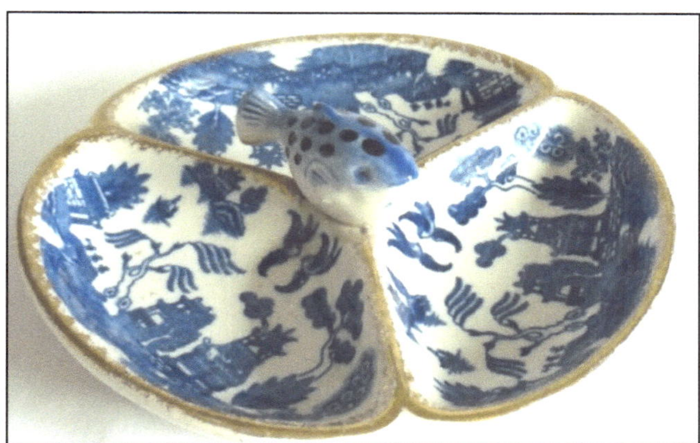

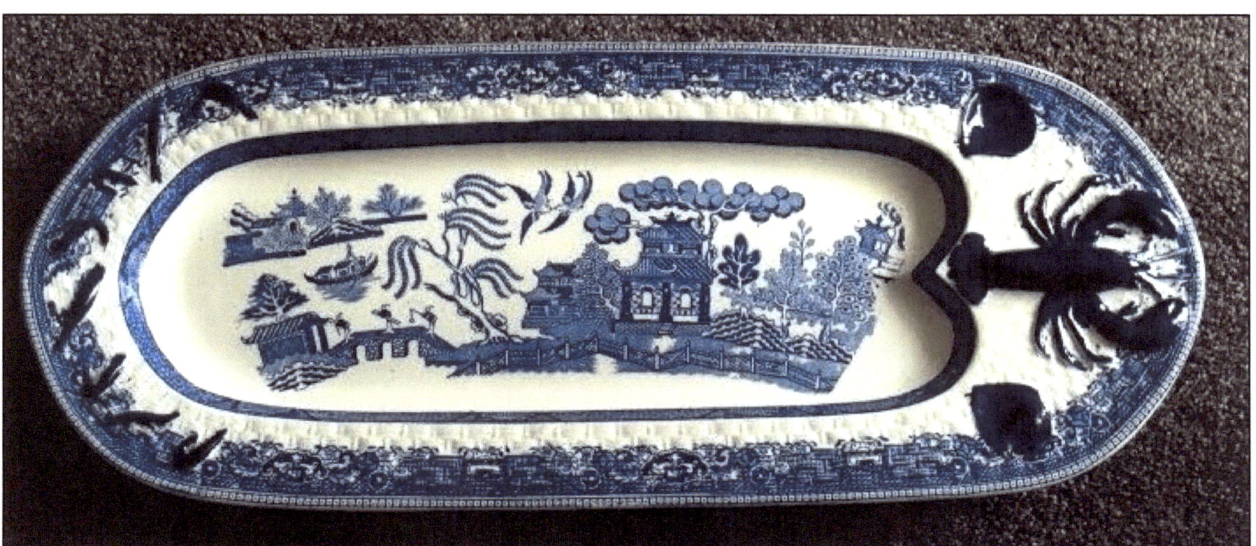

GREETING CARDS

Greeting cards are a great way to communicate important feelings to people that you care about, especially when the card is unexpected and has a special message in it. The Blue Willow Pattern since its creation has featured on numerous cards, here is a selection of cards.

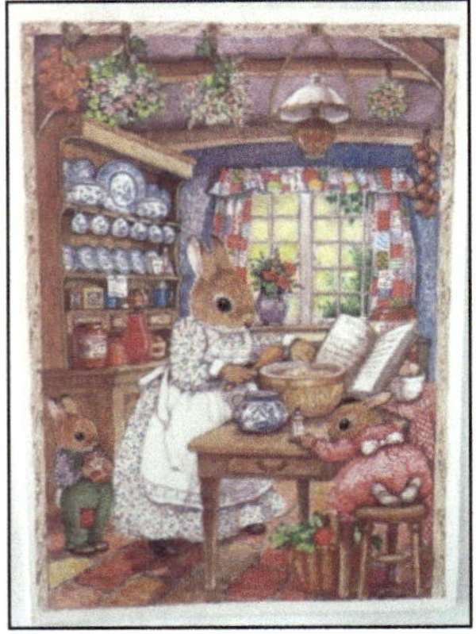
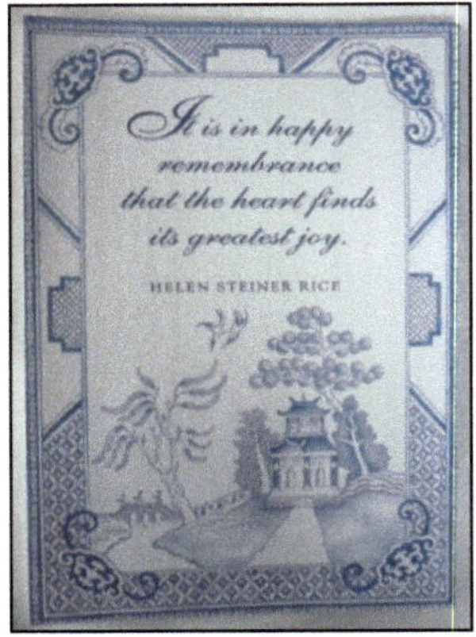

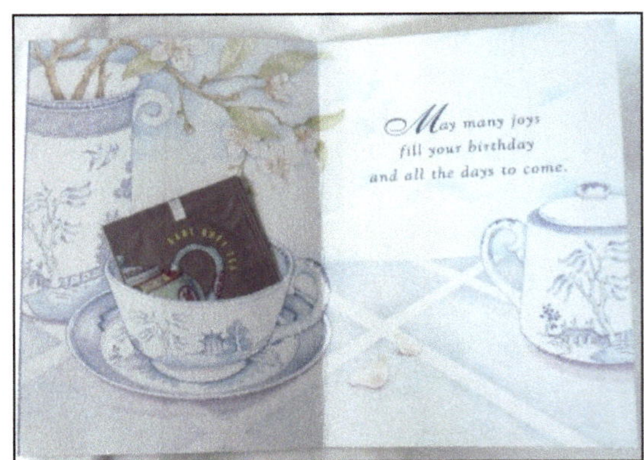

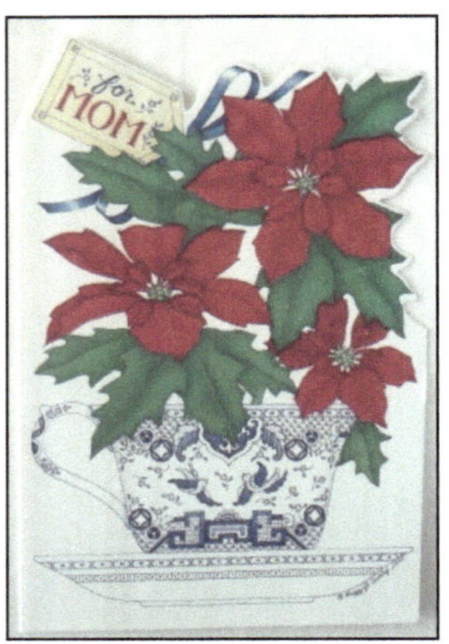

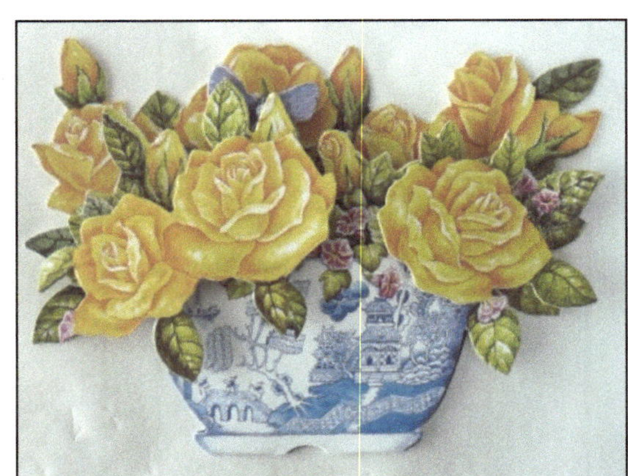
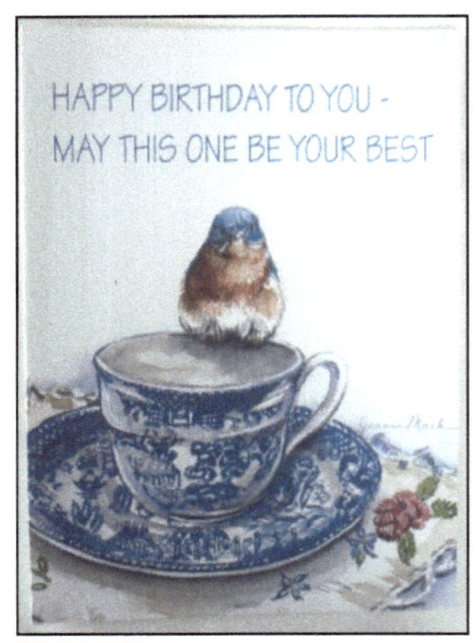

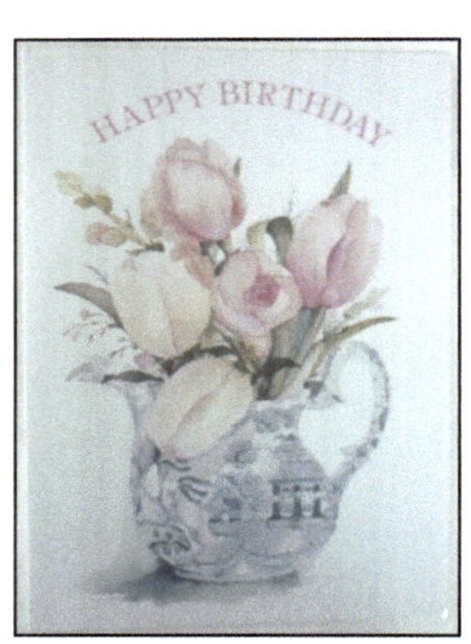

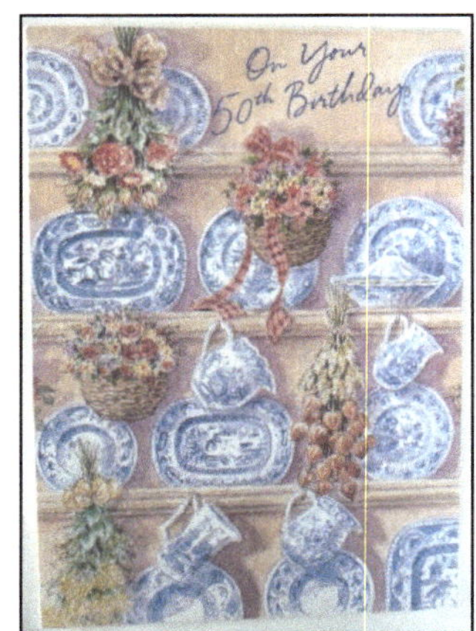

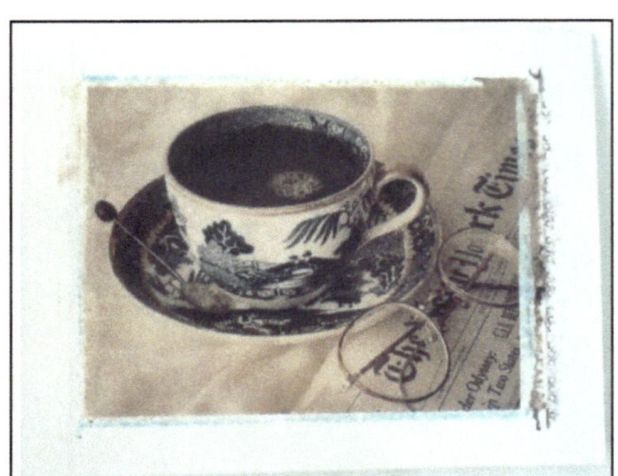

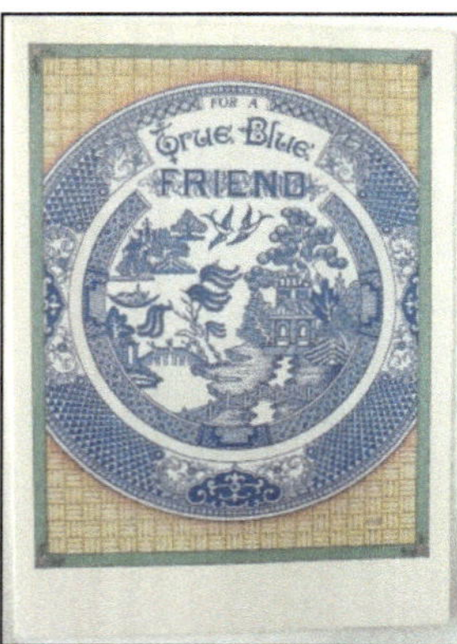

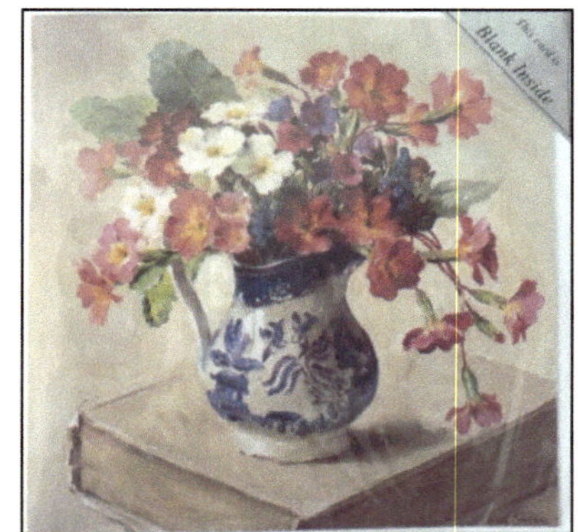
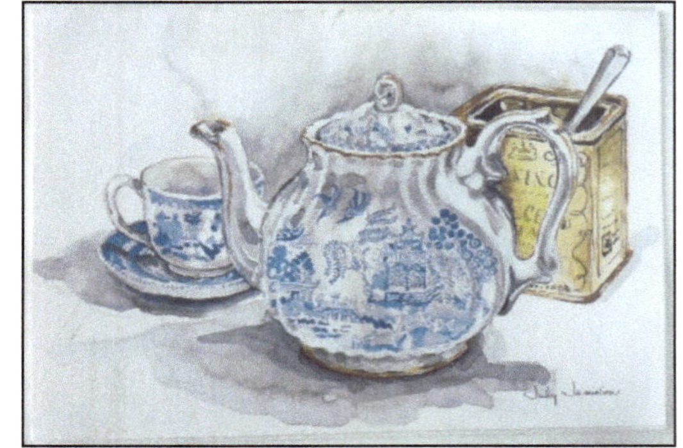

GLASSES

Use of the Blue Willow Pattern on glassware has been quite prevalent over the past thirty to forty years as can be seen from the examples below. Chances are that if you visit your local antique mall you're bound to find a glass with the Blue Willow Pattern on it. The problem with glass as we all know is that it has a high tendency to break when knocked over or dropped, hence finding a complete set of glasses is quite rare.

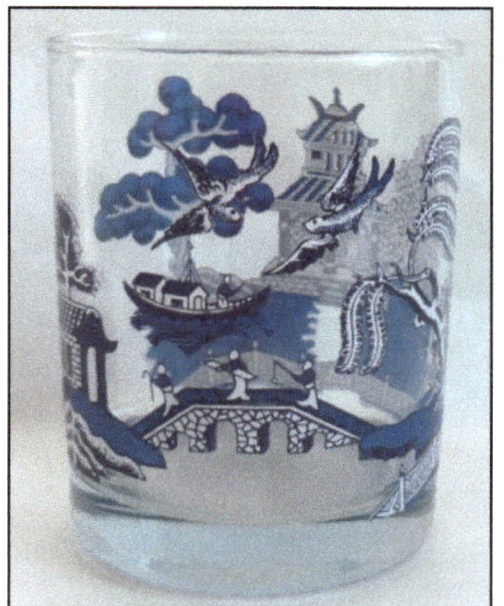
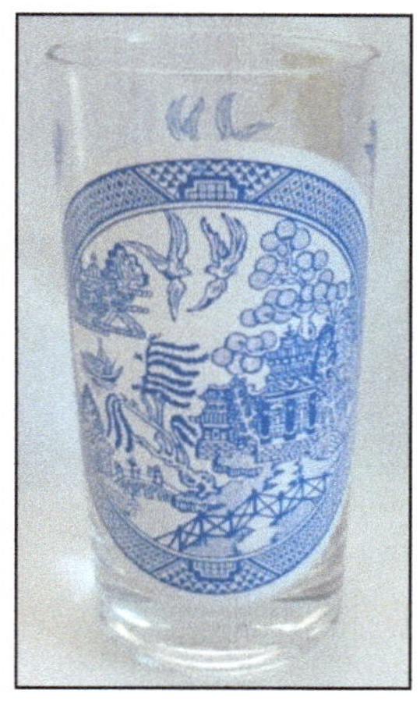
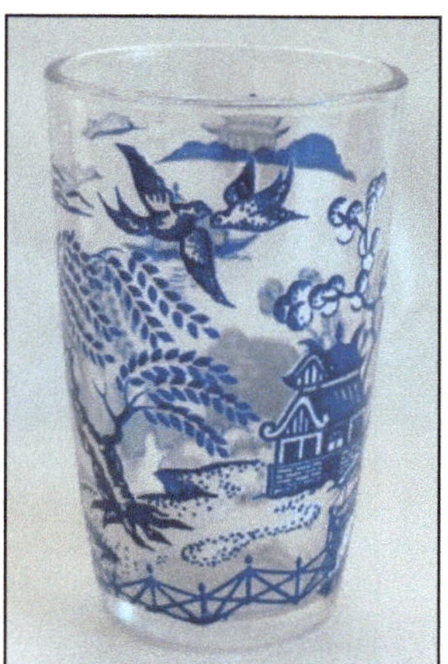
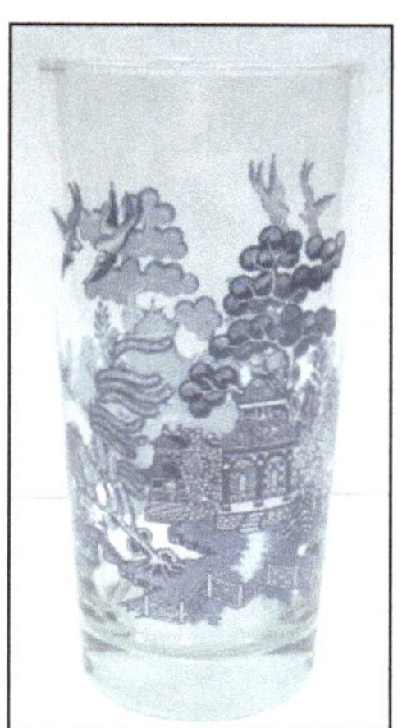

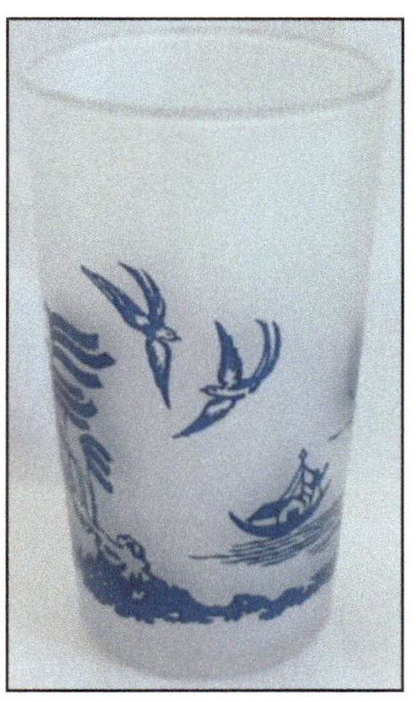
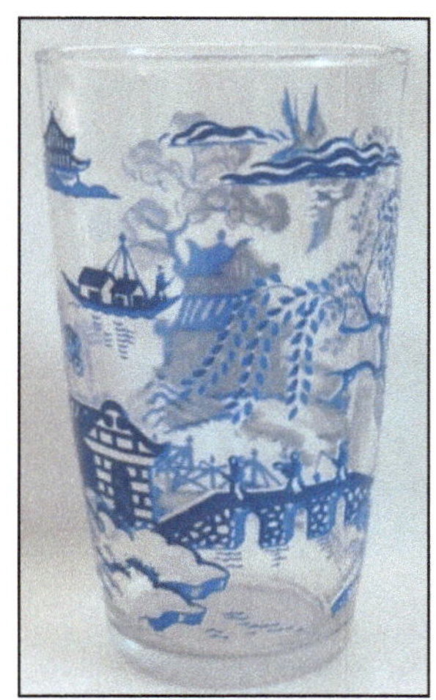
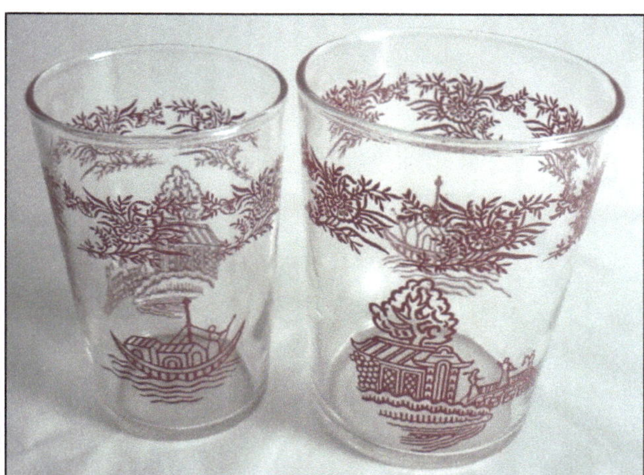

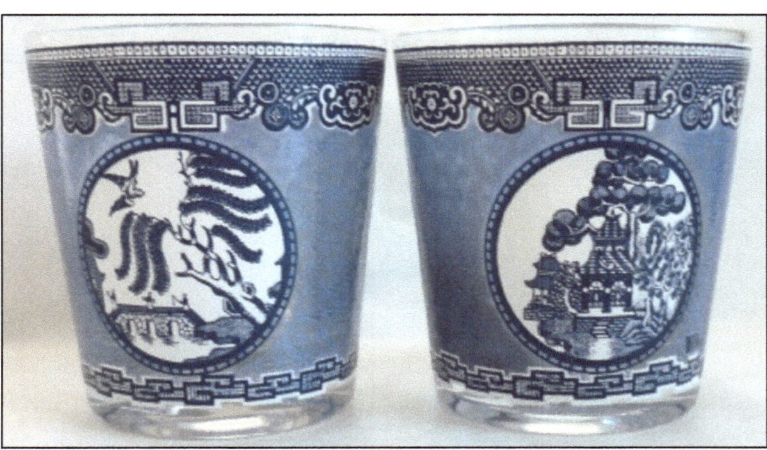
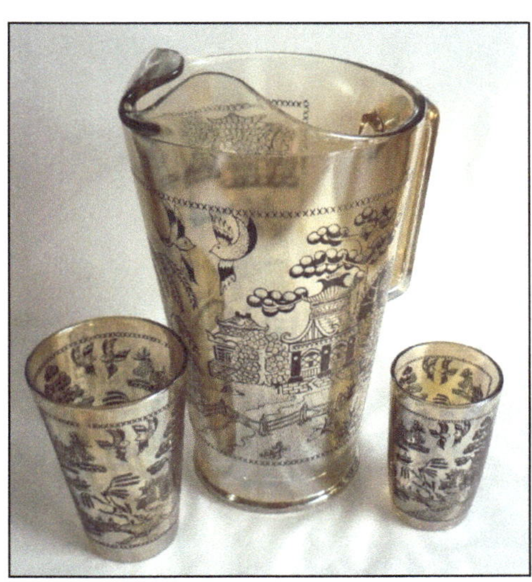

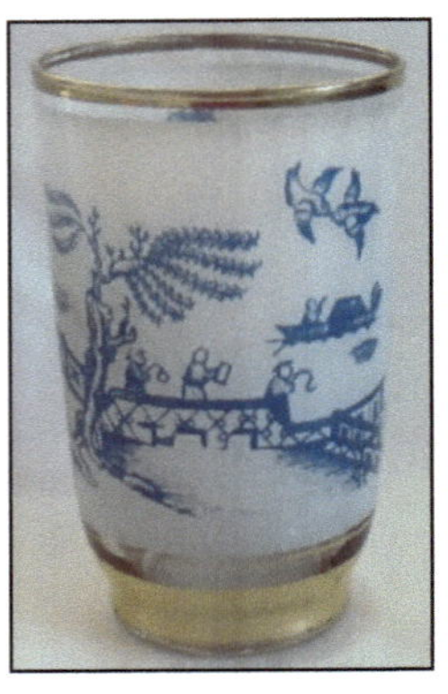 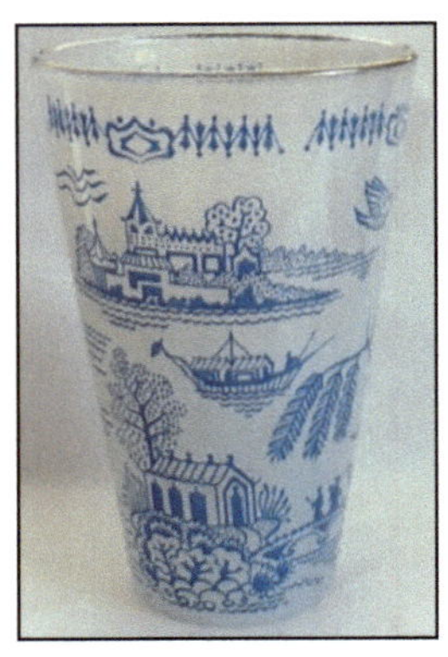 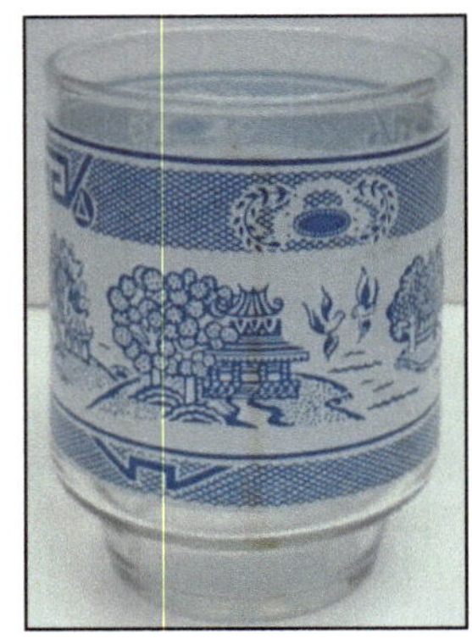 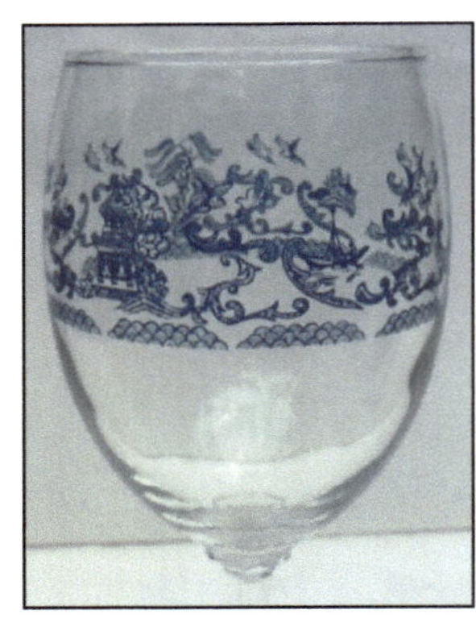

HANDBAGS & SHOES

While I have seen a number of shoes which have been custom made and individually handcrafted, all of the shoes below have been commercially available in recent times. The boot which appears on this page is made by British shoe and boot maker Doctor Martin's and can be bought today (2017) for 120 British Pounds.

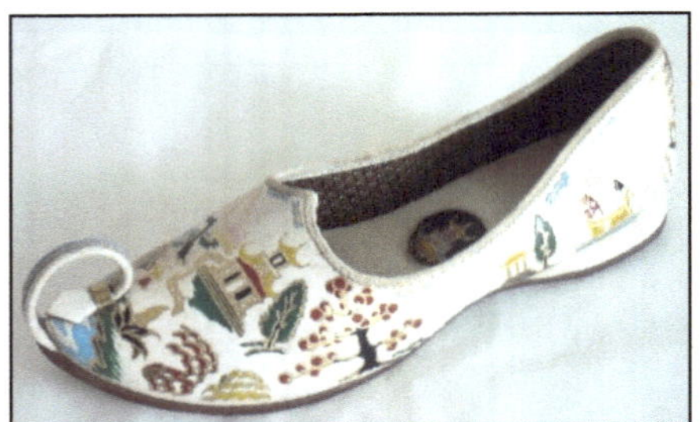 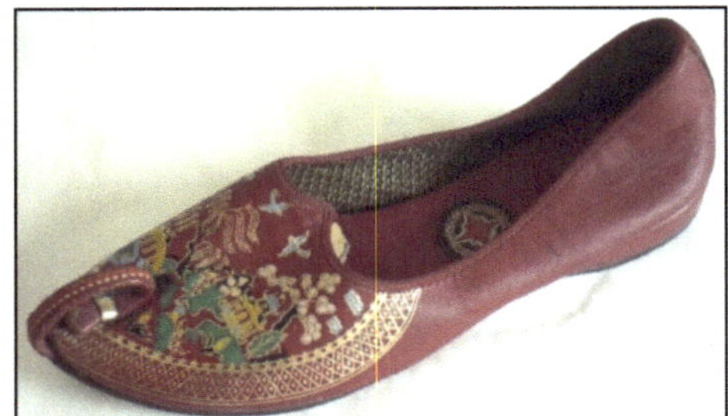 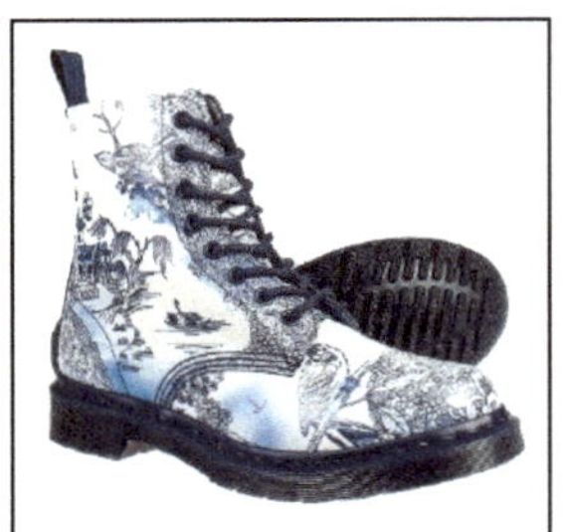

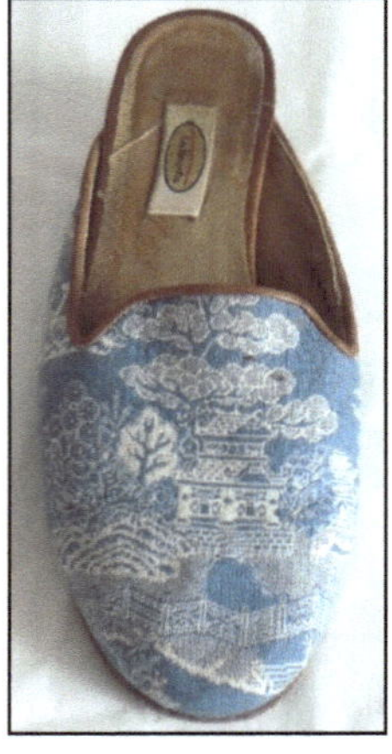 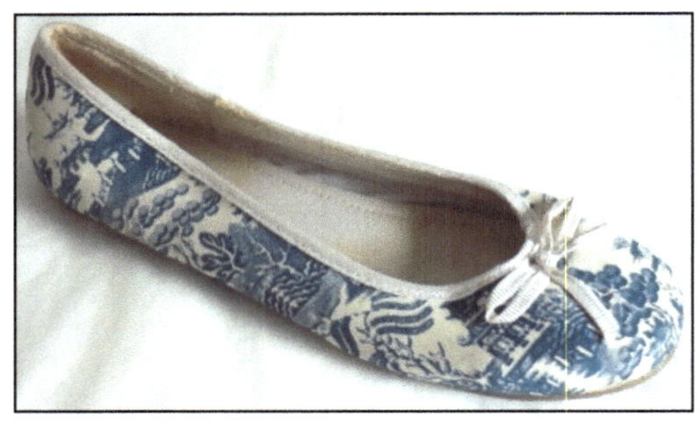 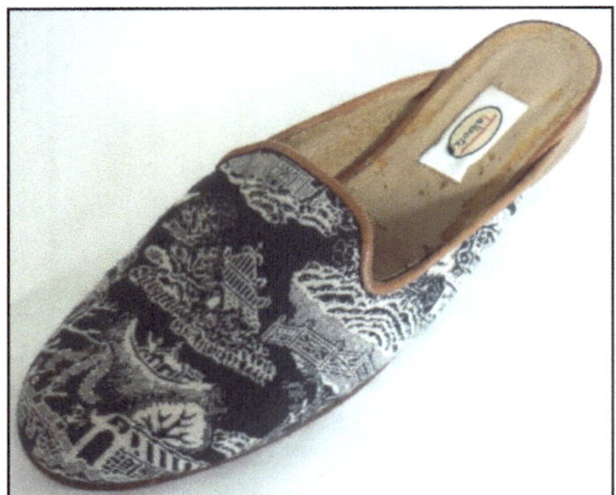

I've included handbags with shoes because as you will see some handbags were made by the same manufacturer, thus enabling the purchaser of the shoes to have matching accessories. Like the shoes, all of these items are from recent times.

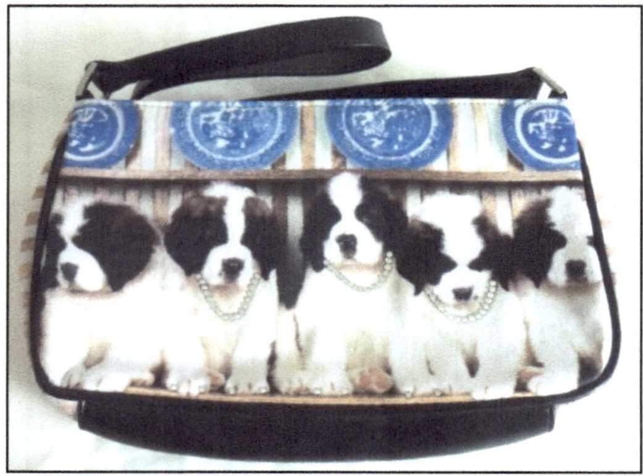 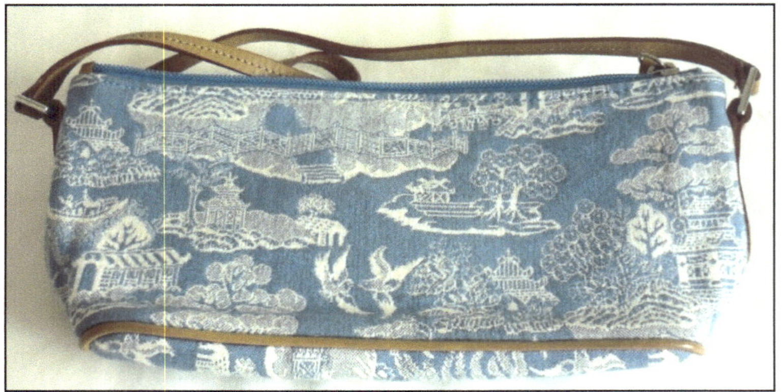

INTERESTING ITEMS

On this page I have put together a collection of interesting items that depending on time (as in history) can be found around the home.

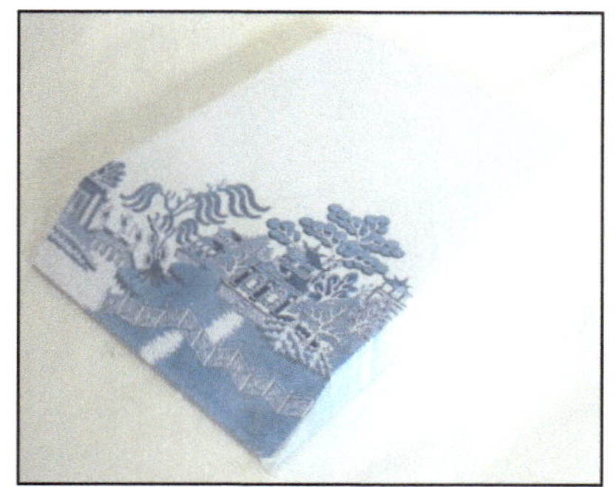

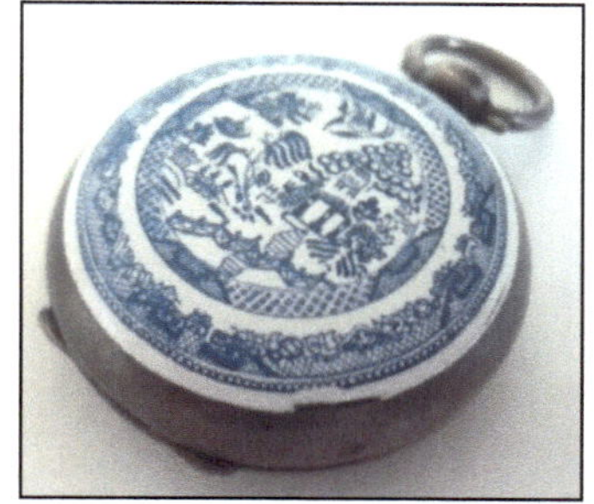

Sovereign case

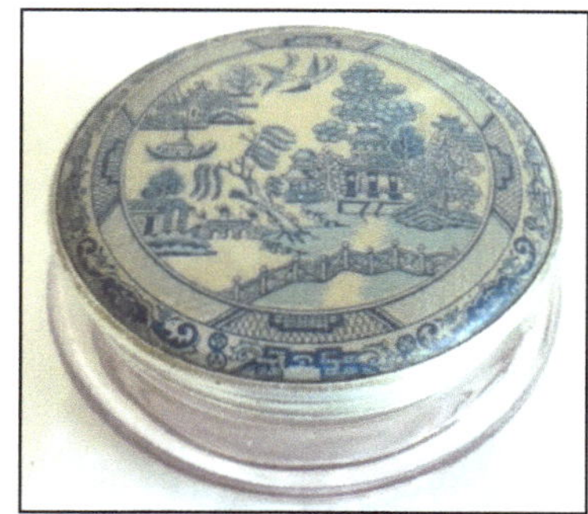

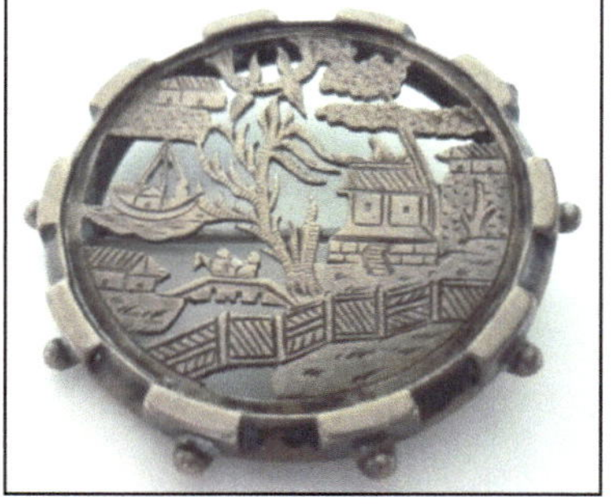

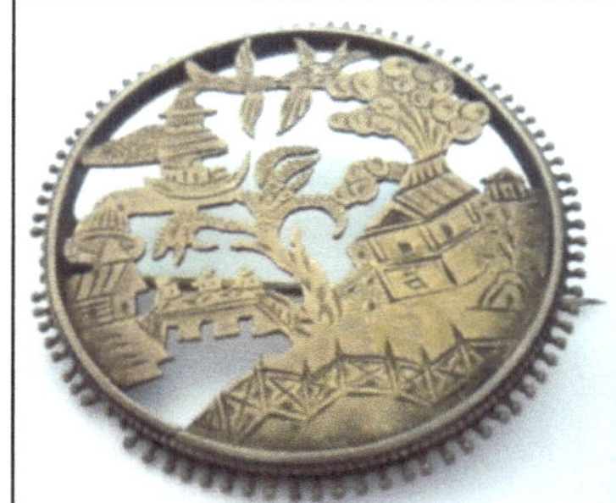

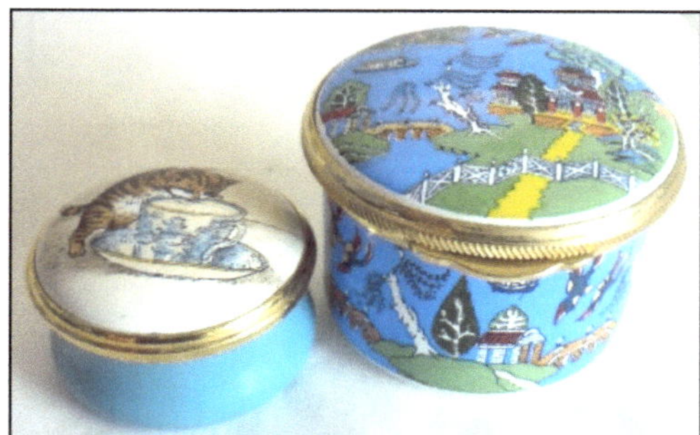

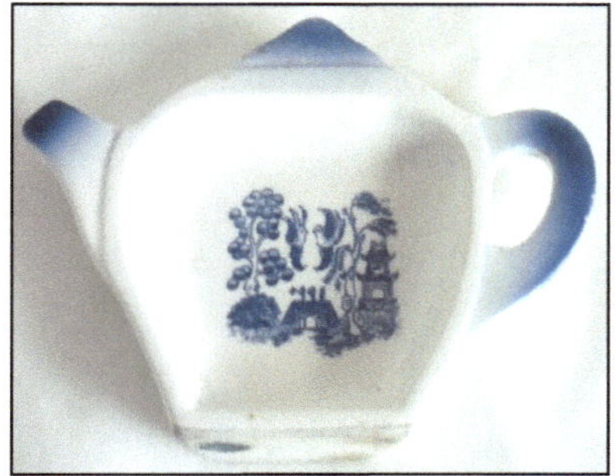

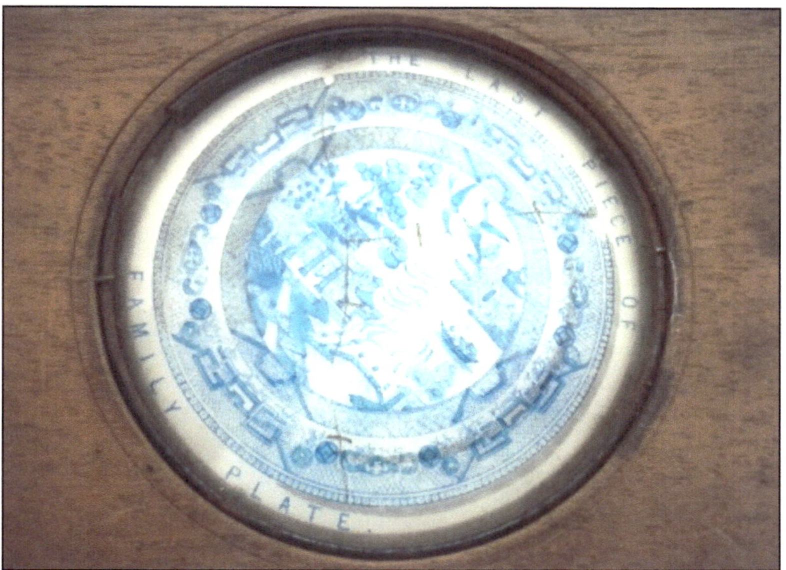

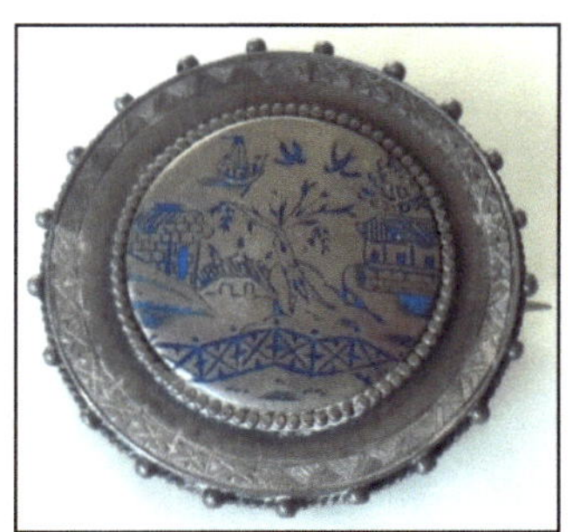

Pictured above, magic lantern slide.

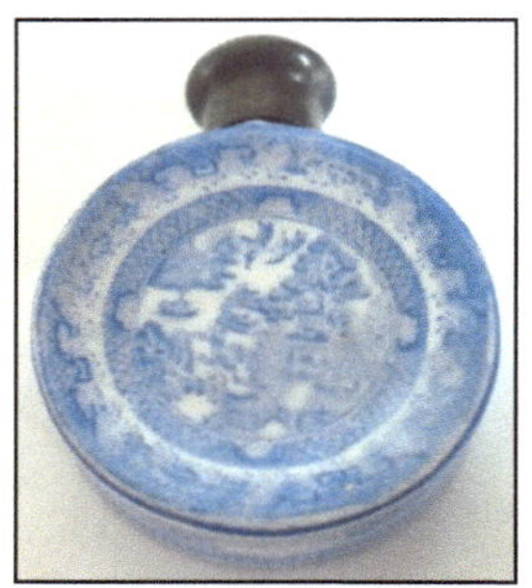

Perfume bottle

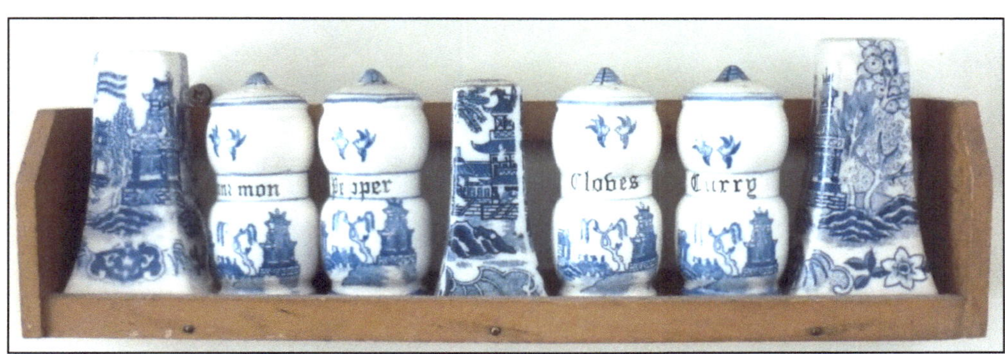

KETTLES & TEAPOTS

Kettles and teapots are virtually part of everyone's day to day life, so much so, there are countless kettles and teapots that have had the Blue Willow Pattern placed on them. There is perhaps scope for a whole book to be dedicated on this subject alone. Here is a brief selection.

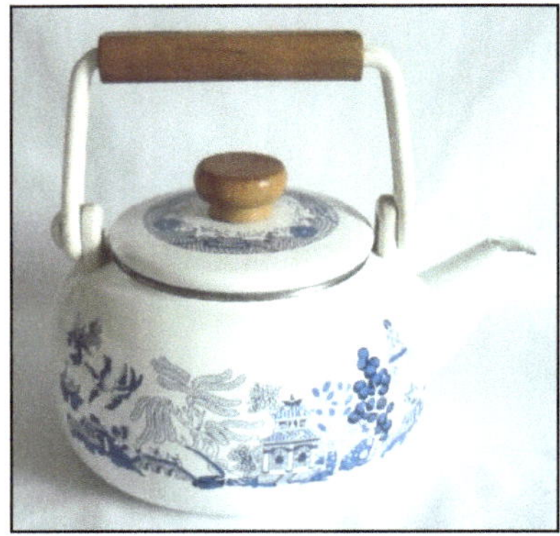
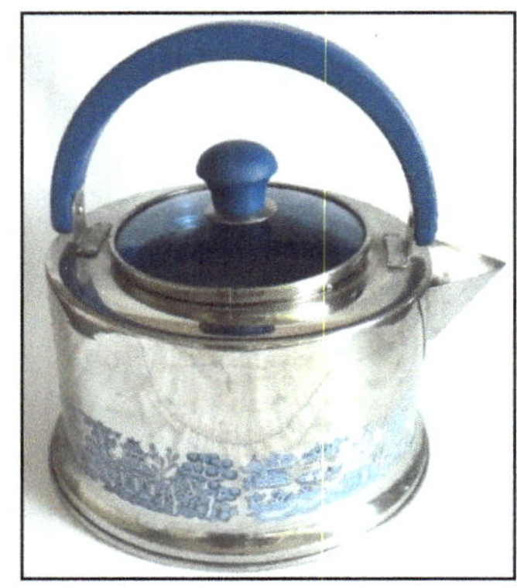
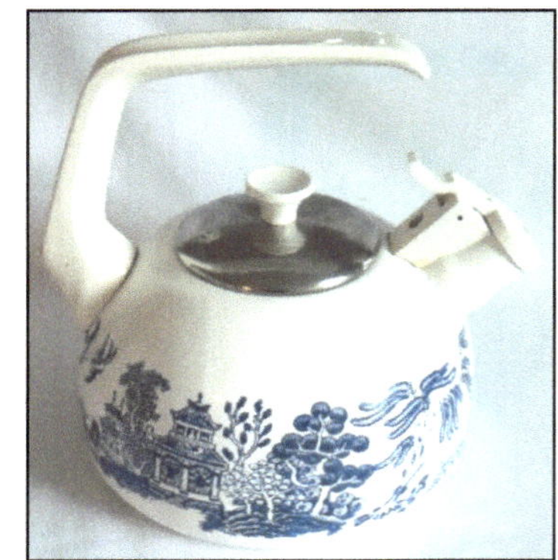

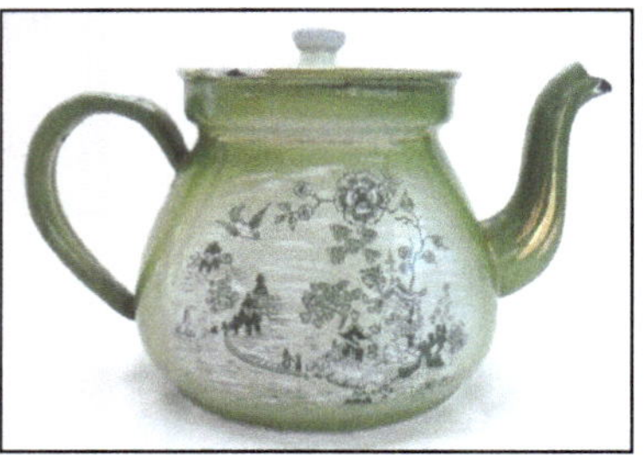
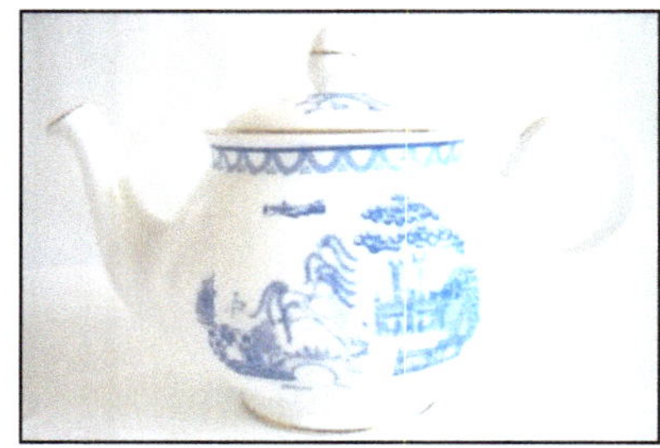
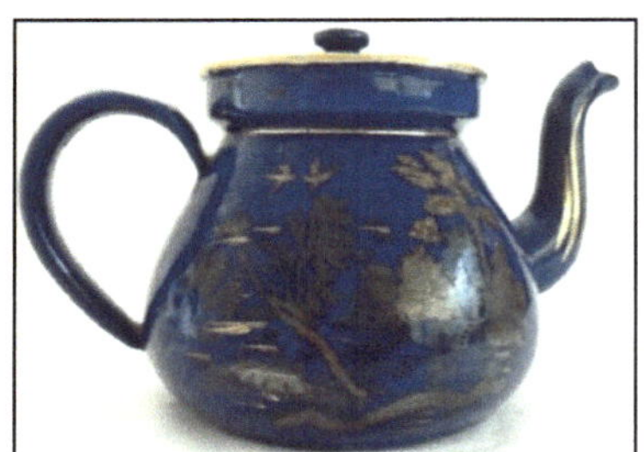

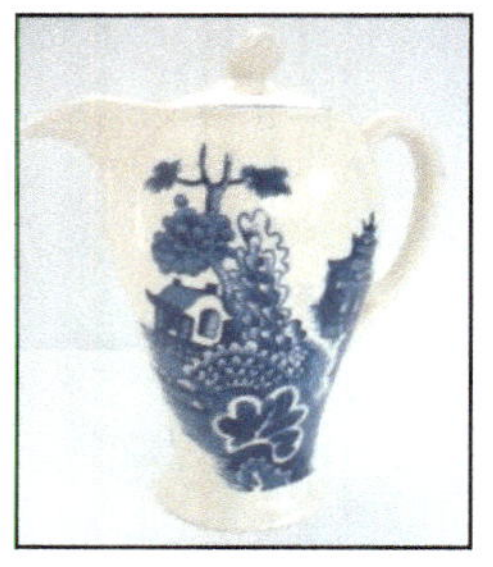
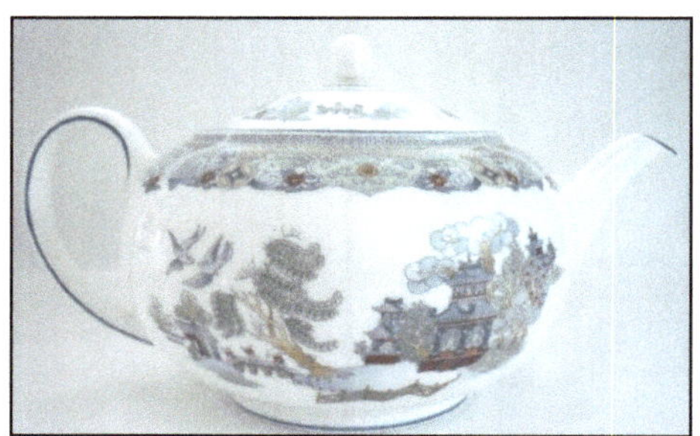
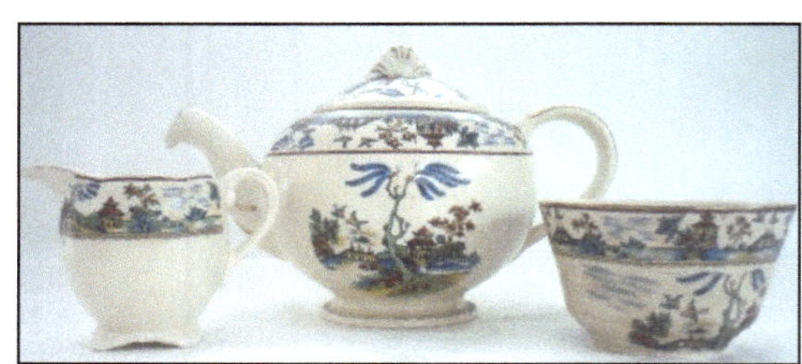

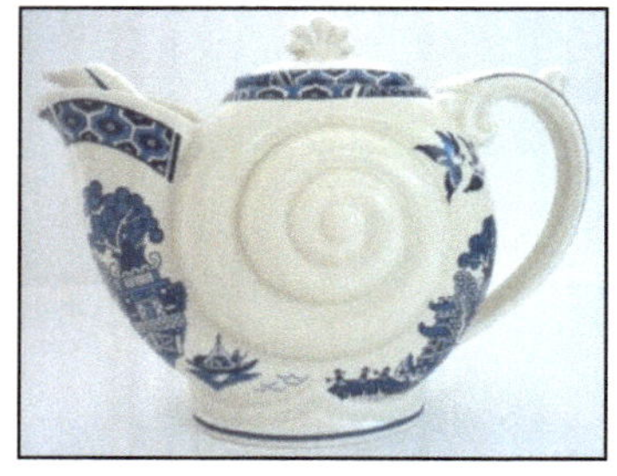
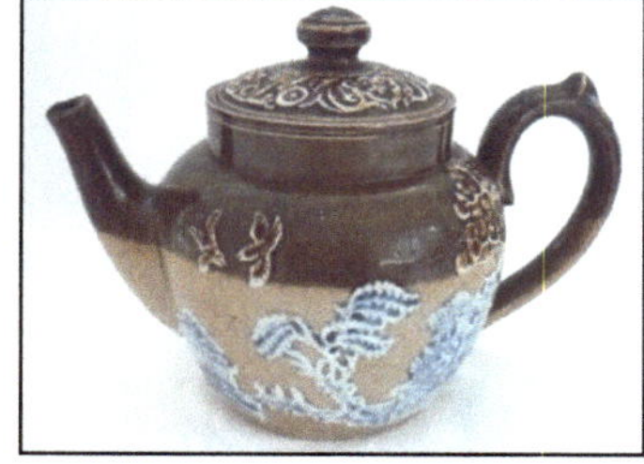
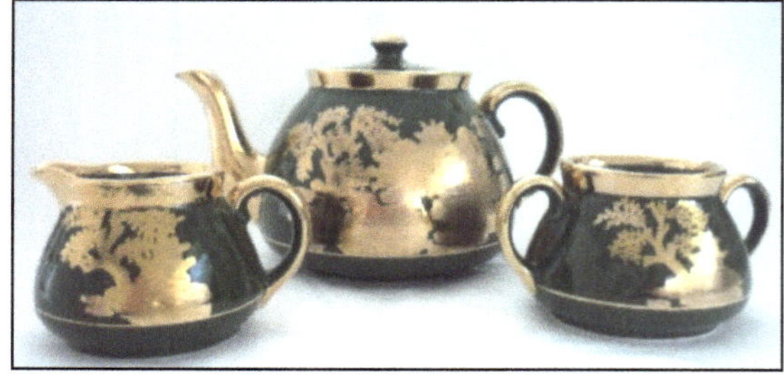

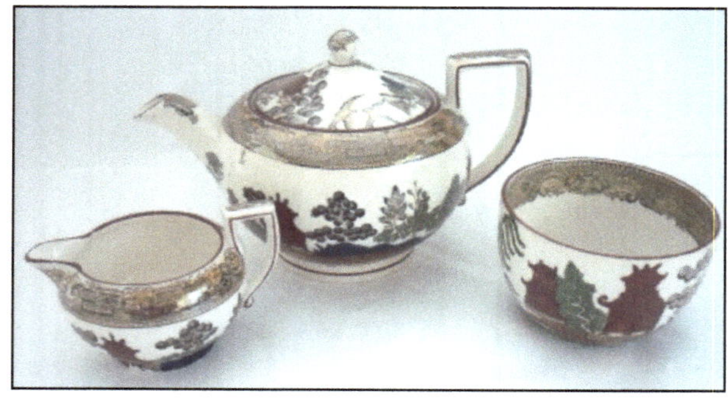
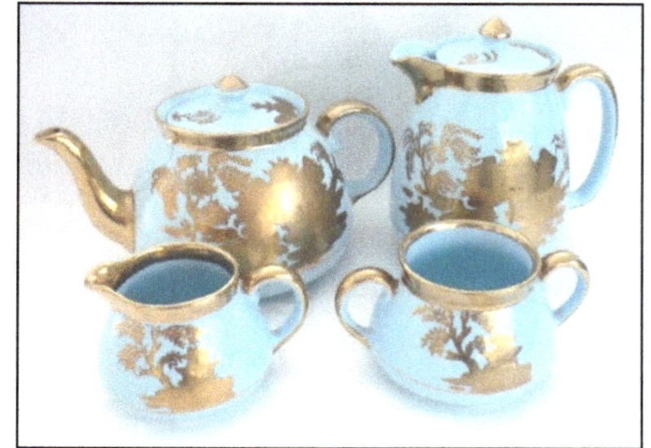

KITCHEN

On this page you'll find a varied selection of items that are commonly found and used in the kitchen.. With several of the pictures I have just shown one item out of a set.

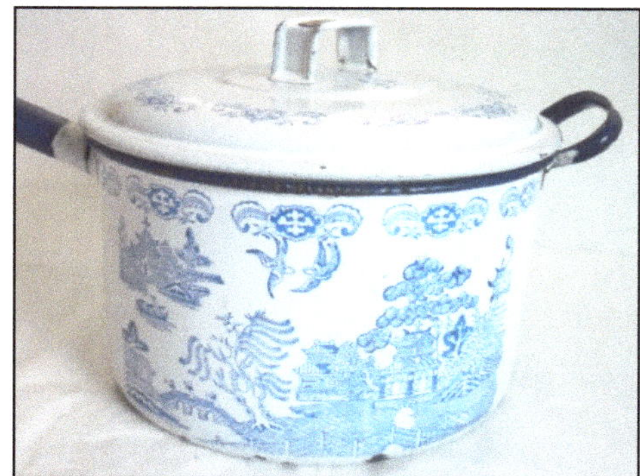

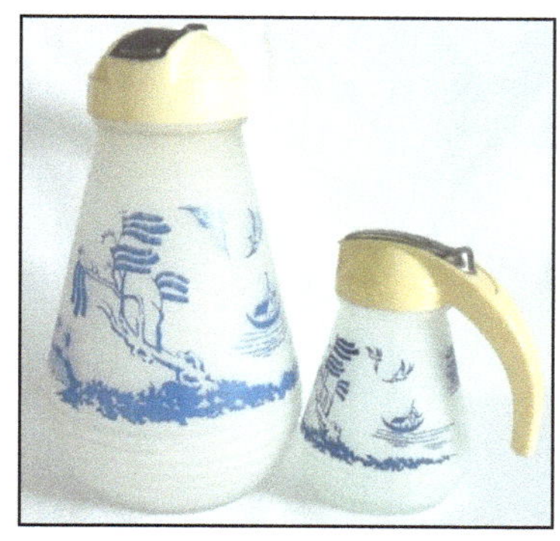

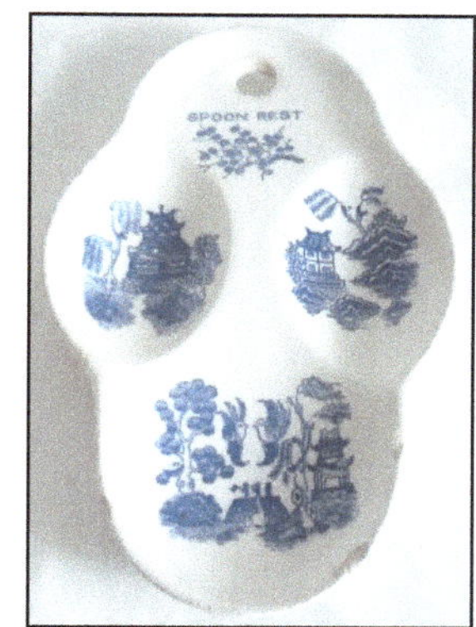

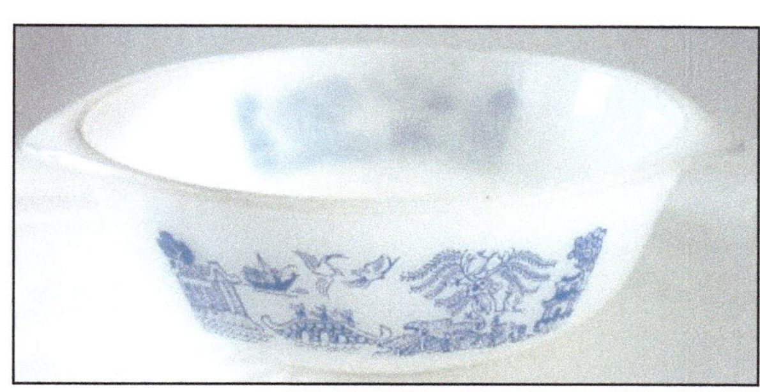

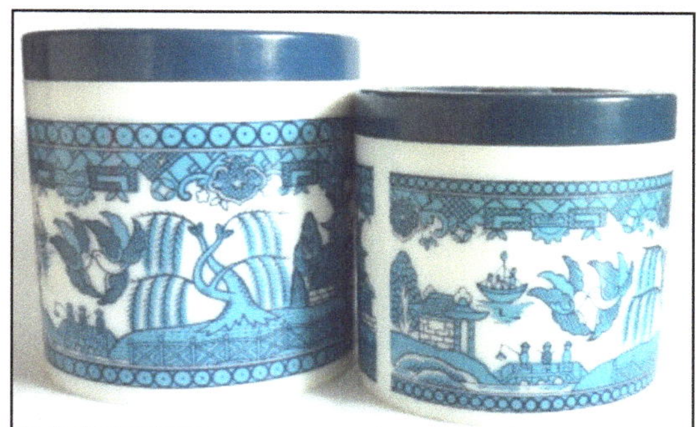

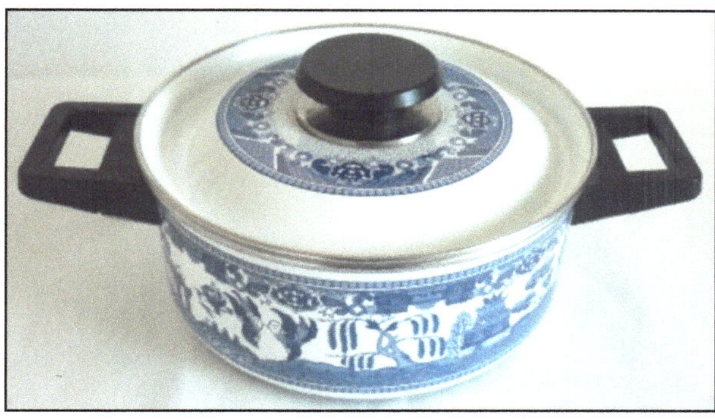

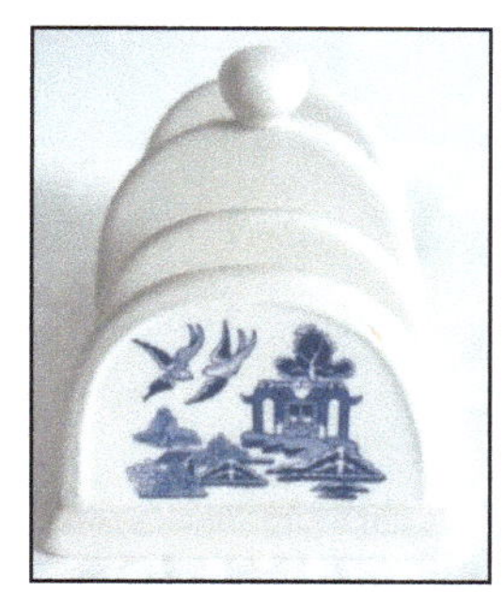

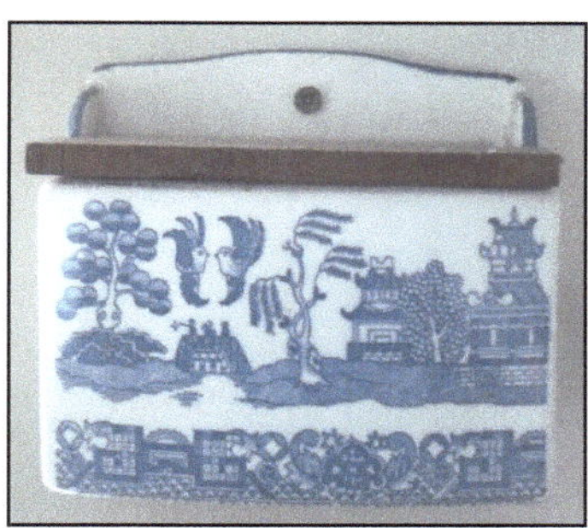

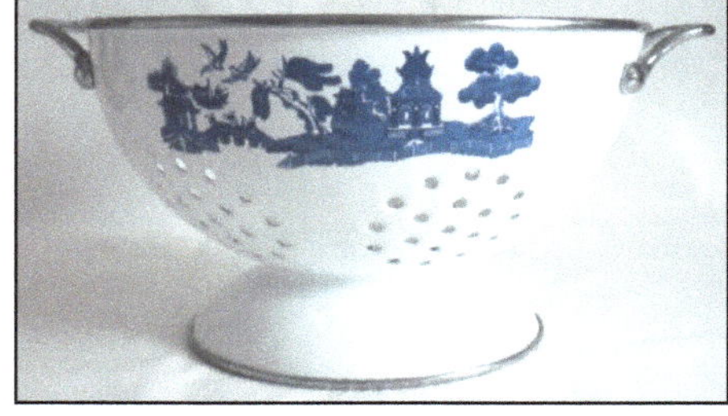

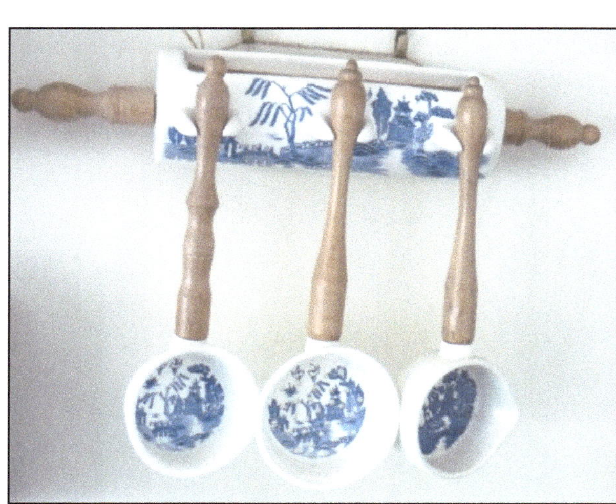

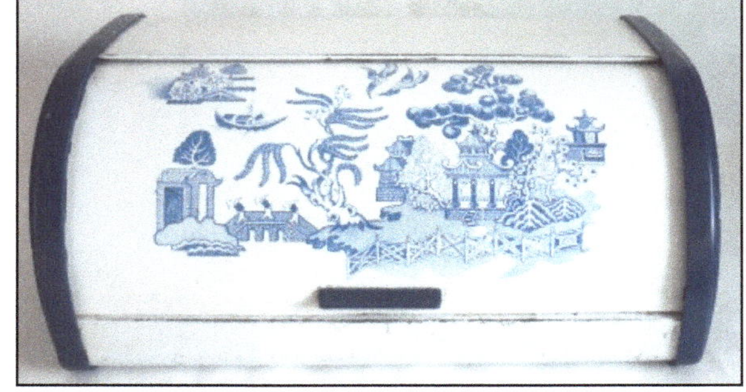

LINEN & TABLECLOTHS

For all of us tablecloths have been a mainstay of our dining experiences, whether it be at home or eating out at a restaurant or diner. Typically a white, or mainly white, tablecloth is used as the standard covering for a dinner table. In the later medieval period spreading a high quality white linen or cotton cloth was an important part of preparing for a feast in a wealthy household. Over time the custom of arranging tableware on a cloth became common. As eating habits changed in the 20th century, a much greater range of table-setting styles developed. Some formal dinners still use white tablecloths, often with a damask weave, but other colours and patterns are possible. Of course when you mention patterns and colours, then use of the Blue Willow Pattern in many colours over the years has been an obvious choice for many. Here is a selection.

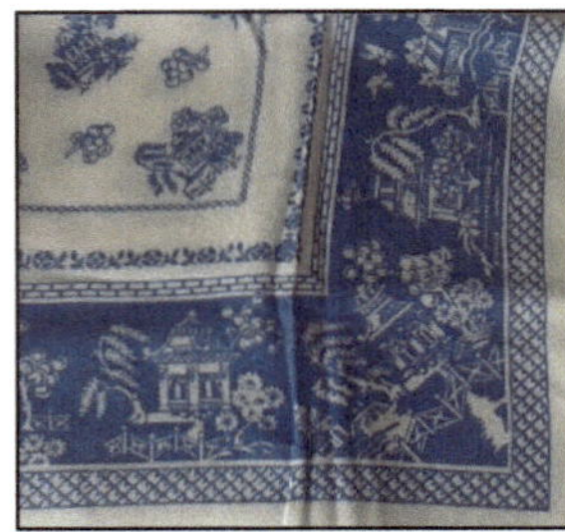
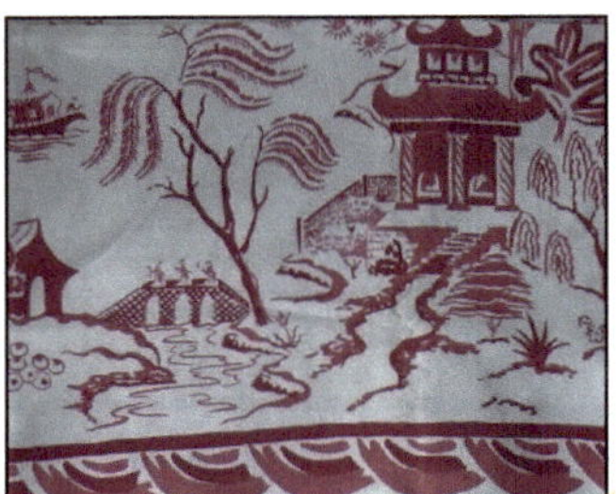
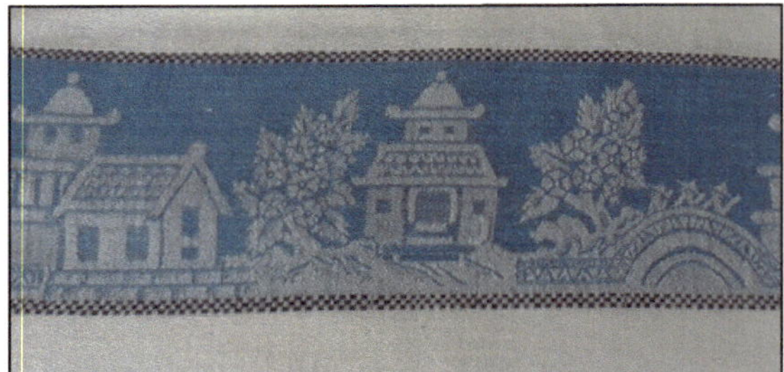

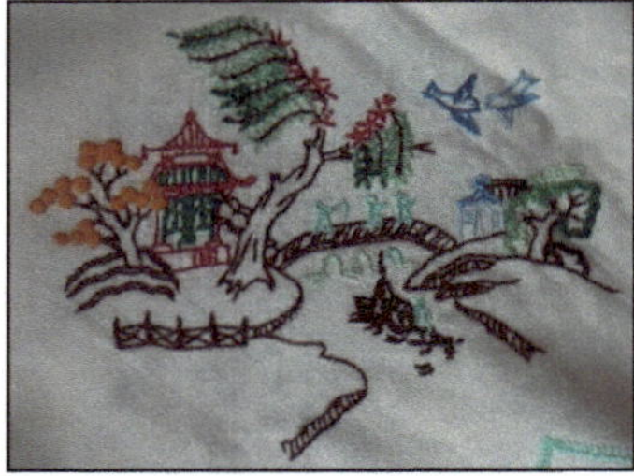
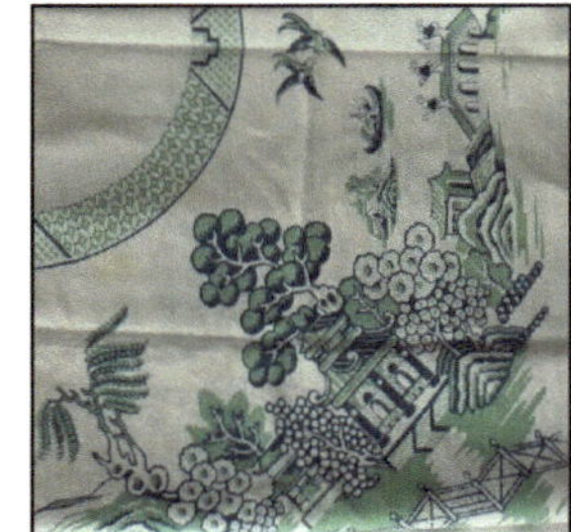
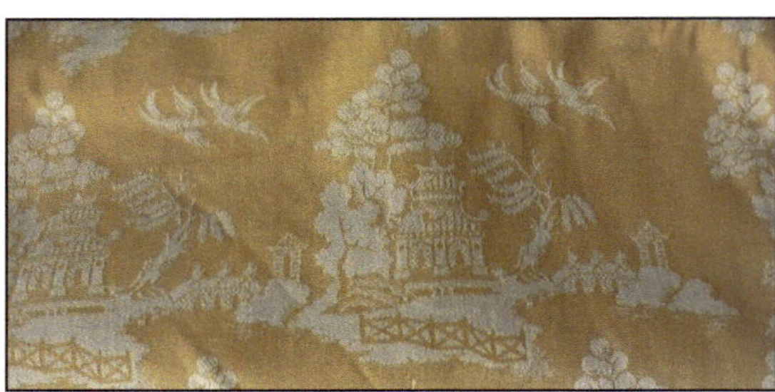

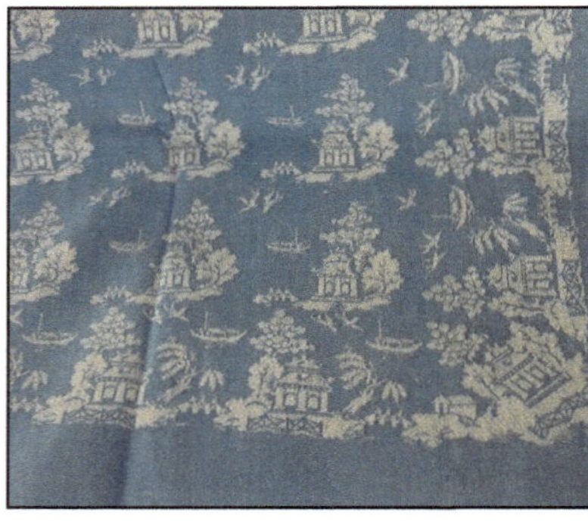
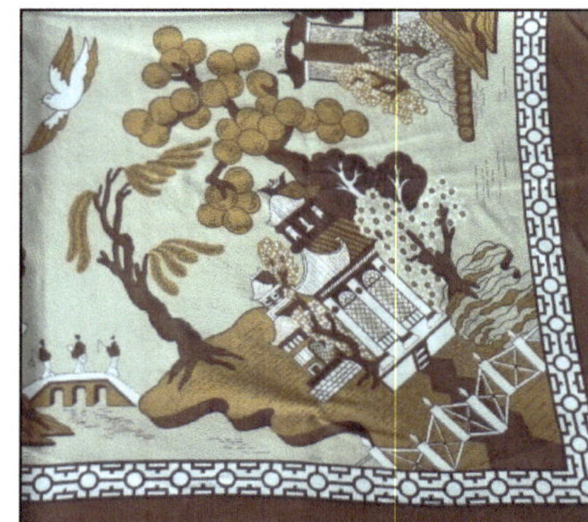
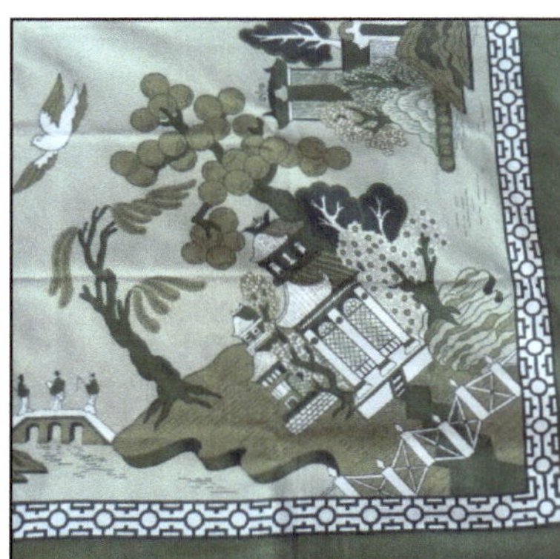

MEAT DRAINERS STRAINERS

From the early 19th century, most dinner sets included a drainer, or mezzanine as they are often called, which was flat and had a hole in the center, with smaller holes all around it. This drainer would fit inside a large serving dish and would have been used when serving meat and fish, to drain the juices.

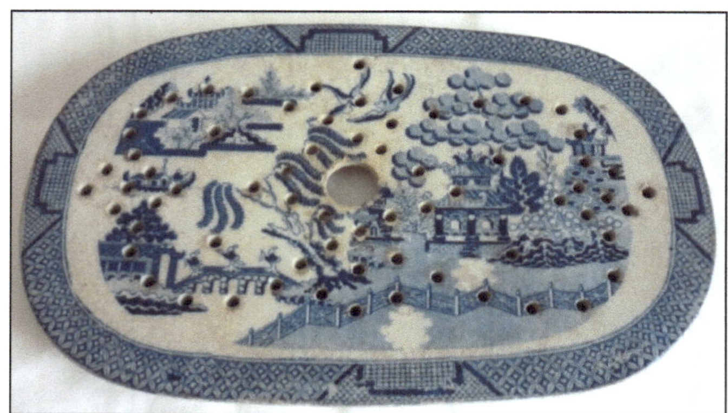
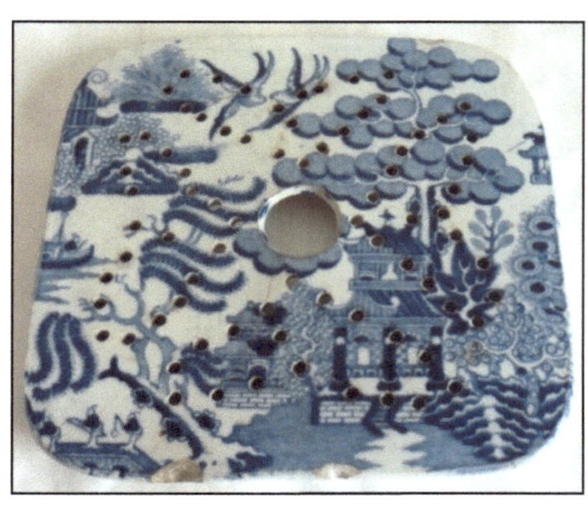

METALWARE

Many forms of metalware using the Blue Willow Pattern can be found around the house. Several examples of these are also shown in individual categories throughout this book, these include tins, baking and kitchen items to name a few. On this page are items which could have a particular category, however I have selected a broad selection of different items to represent metalware in general. Some of the items are brass, silver, others are plated silver and some are tin. The age of items covers a range of at least 100 years, the older items being the silver plated ones such as the hairbrush and the soap box, with new items being the tin tray and small silver picture holder. All the items show the Blue Willow Pattern. On some items like the small brass tray this is impressed, on others it is etched into the metal and on the hairbrush and small box it is raised, so that it is almost three dimensional. On the tray the pattern is applied by way of lithograph.

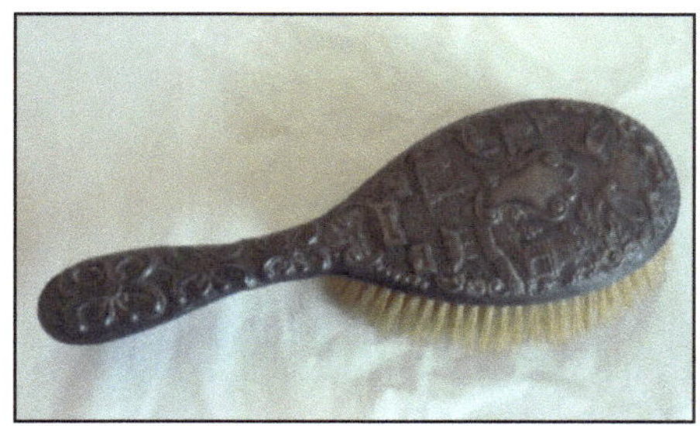
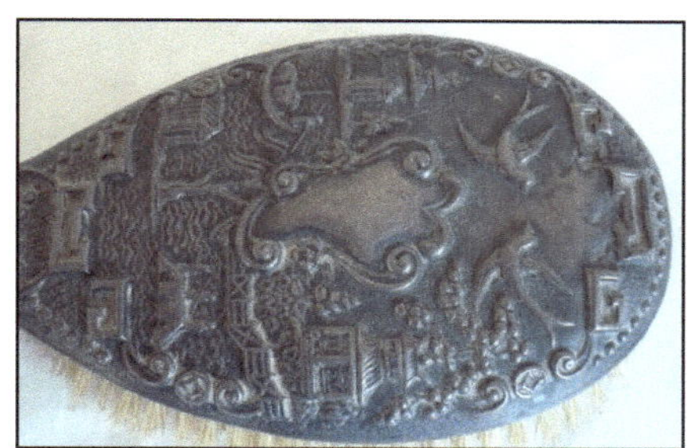
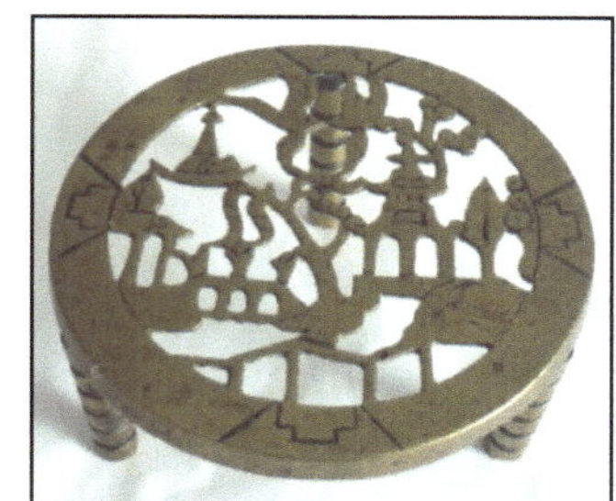
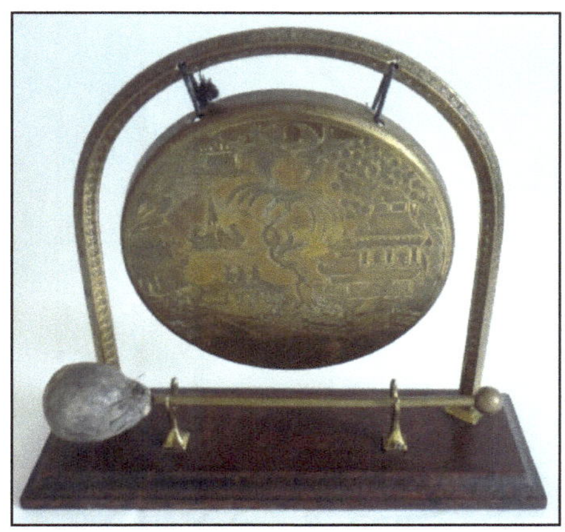
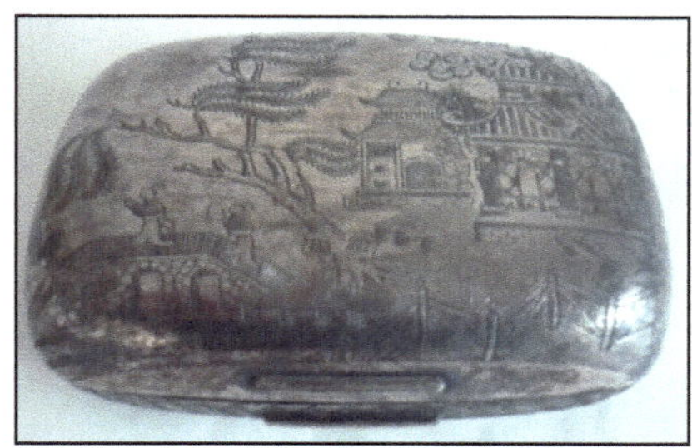
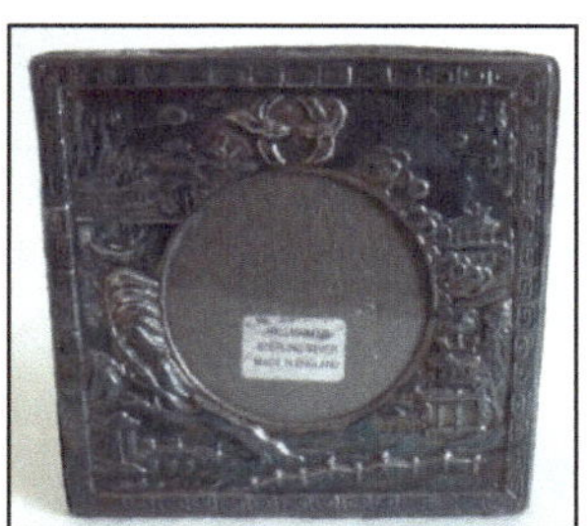
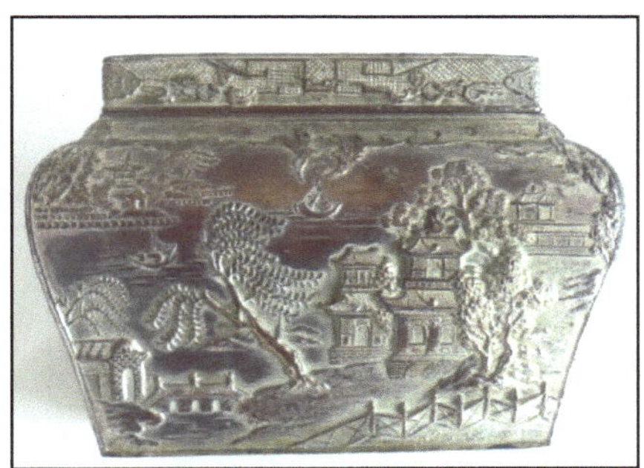
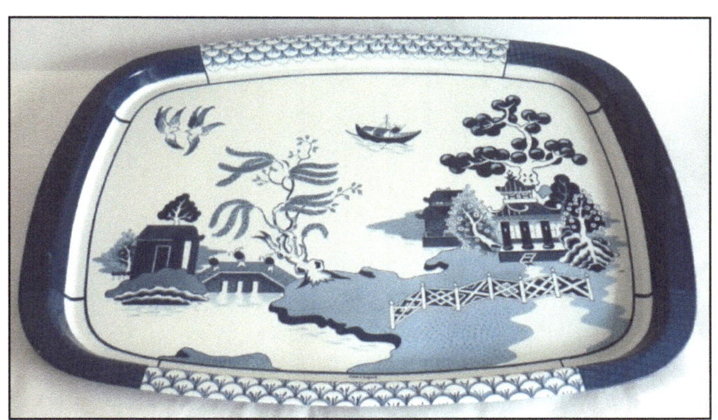
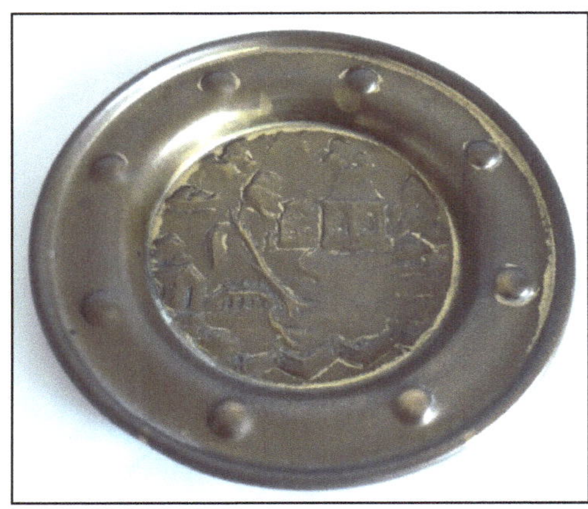
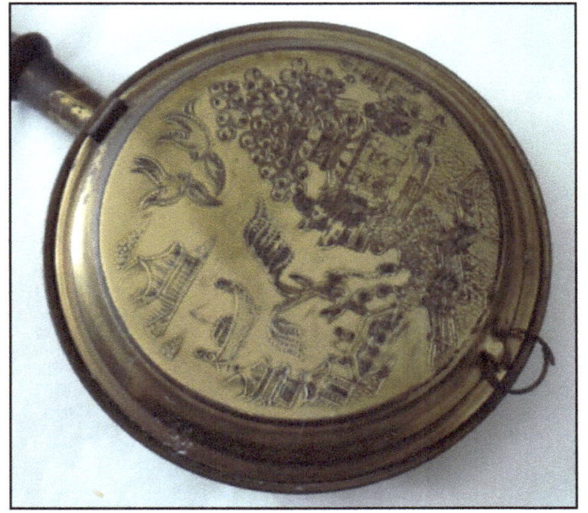

MUGS

The Blue Willow Pattern is not lost on mugs. A mainstay of everyday life, mugs as we know them today have been around since 6,000 BC. There are avid collectors of mugs and there are those who love to be surrounded by mugs. With the exception of the mug on the bottom row to the left showing a scene from Buster Brown, all of the mugs are from recent times. Indeed being ever popular, one does not have to look far to find a mug.

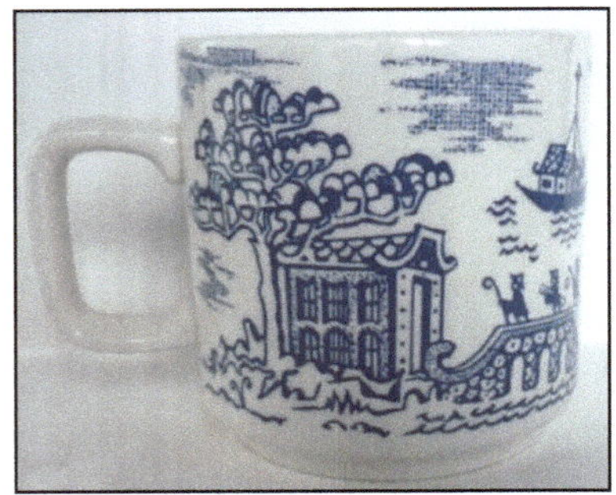
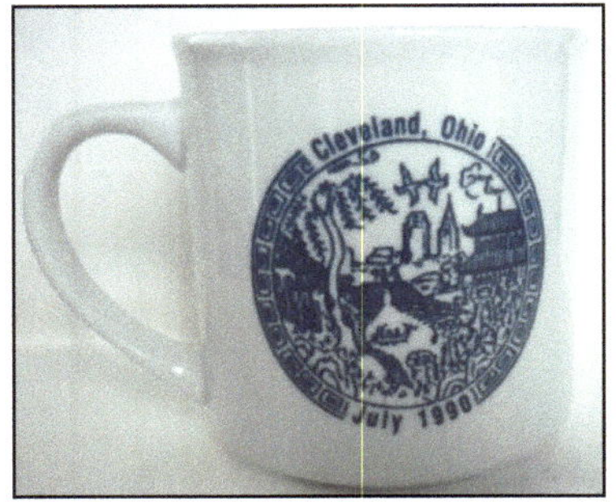
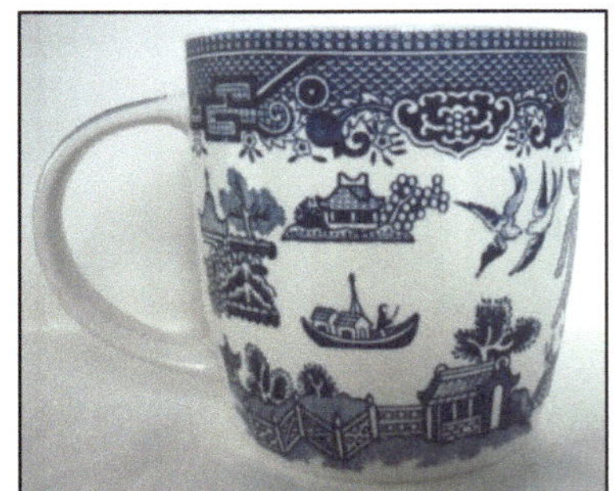
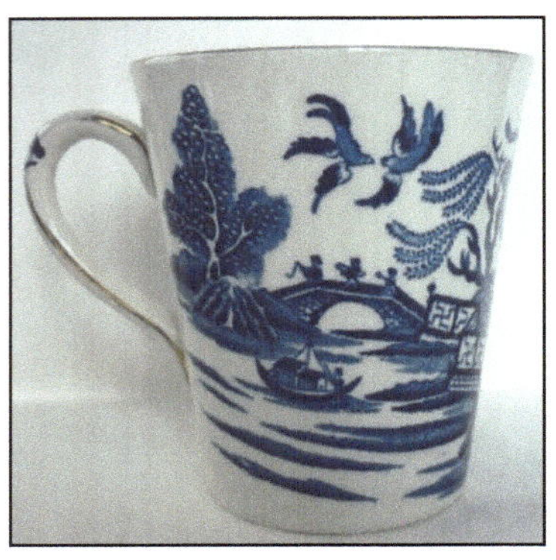
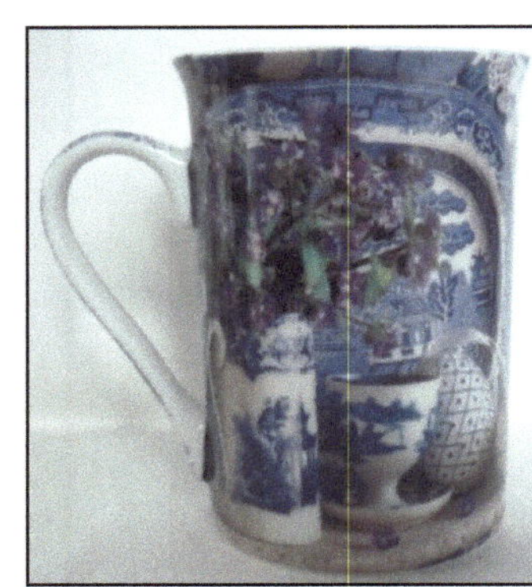
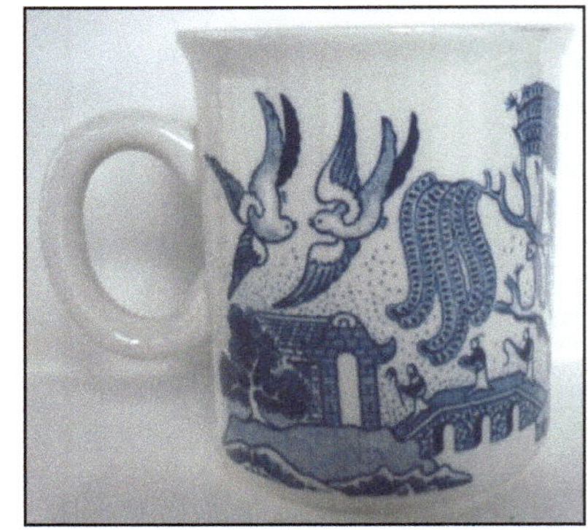
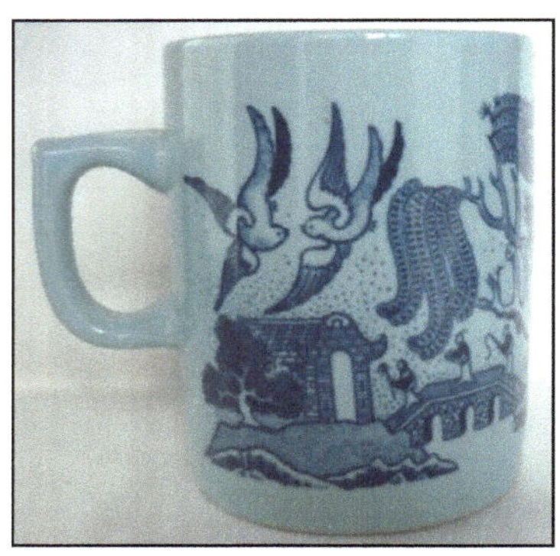
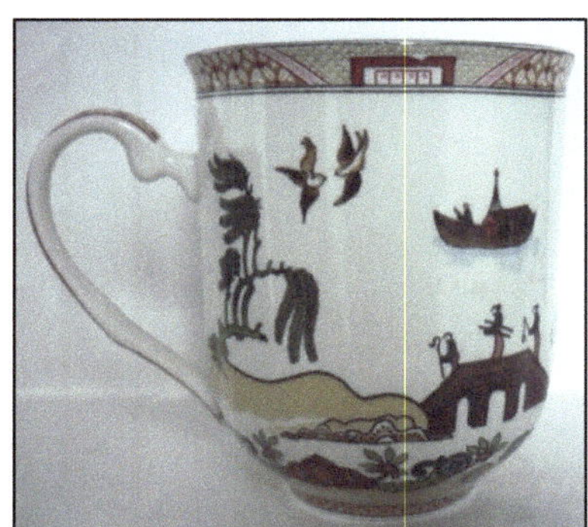
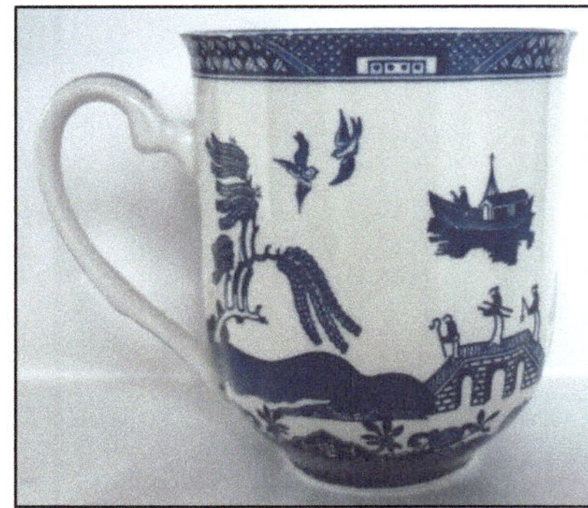
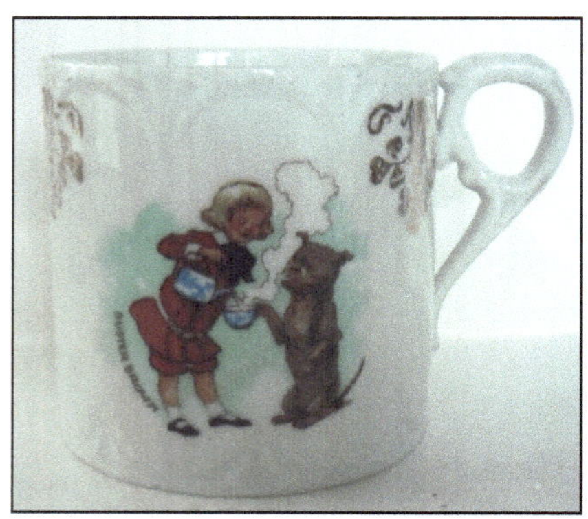
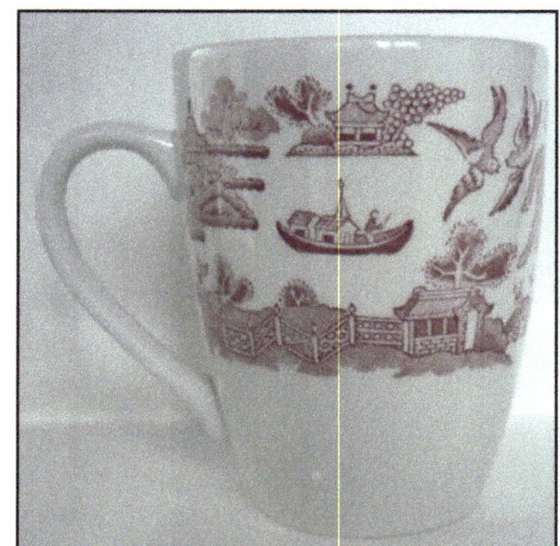
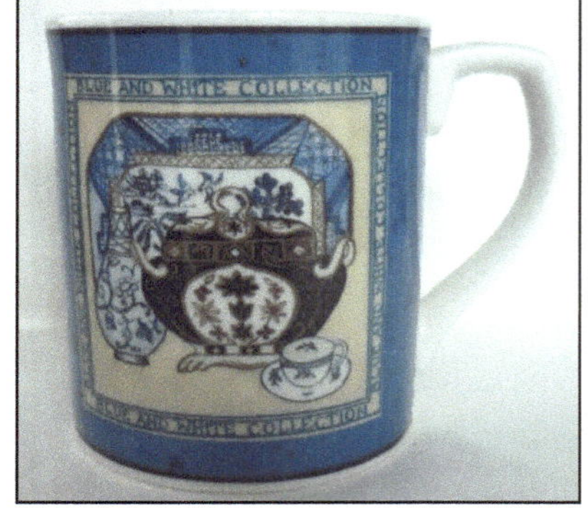

PAINTINGS

Ever since the creation of the Blue Willow Pattern there have been countless artists who have used the pattern as an inspiration for their work. Sometimes as seen in these examples the main focus of the picture is the Blue Willow Pattern as a whole, in others it might be that the pattern makes a cameo appearance , perhaps in the form of a cup and saucer in a larger picture.

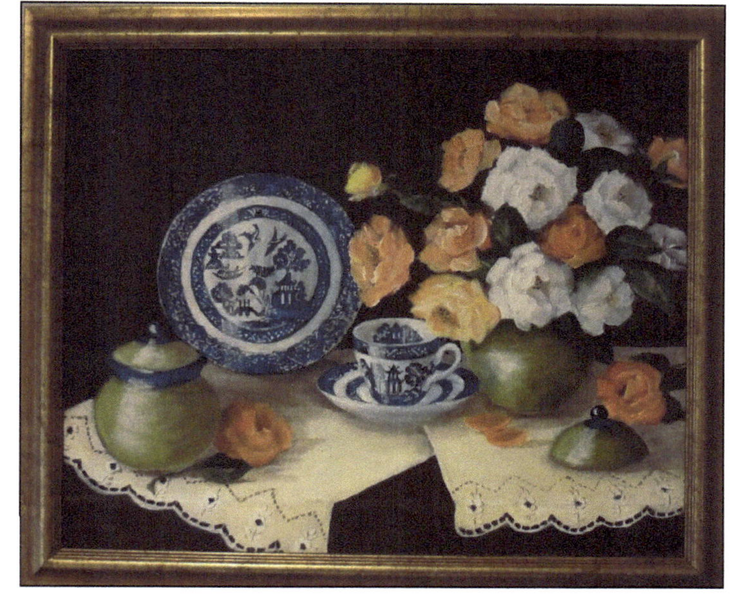

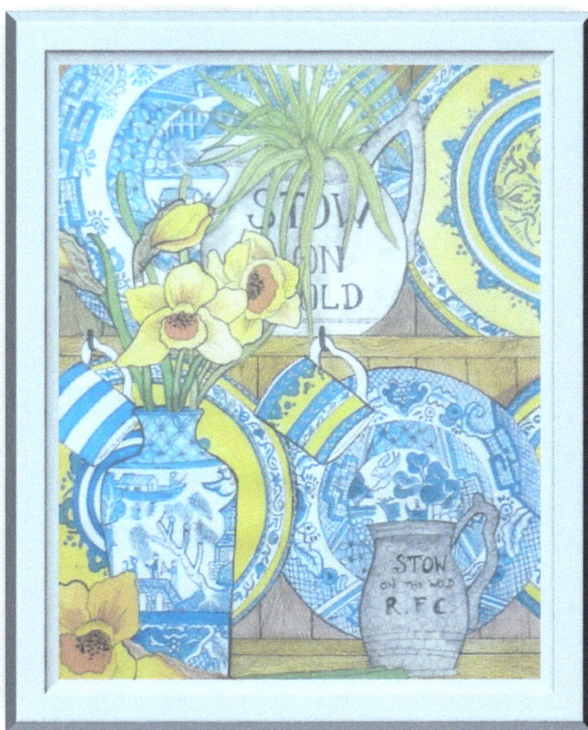

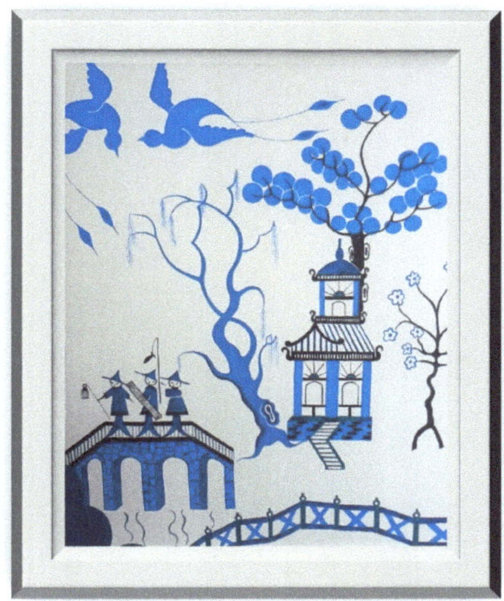

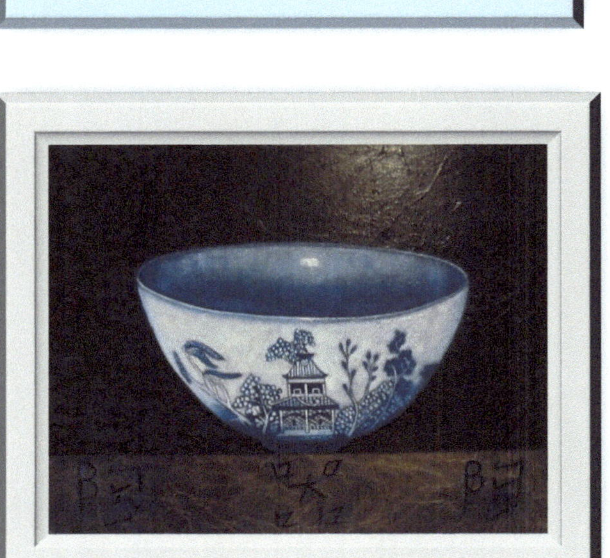

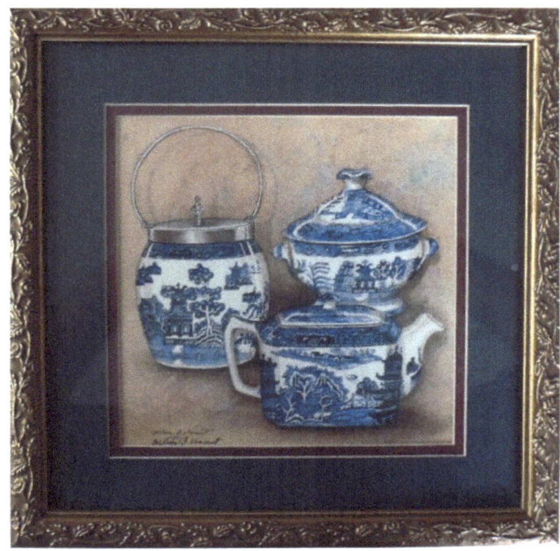

PAPER

My first thoughts about the Blue Willow Pattern being used with paper did not amount to much, that was until I started looking around at what was at hand. Like many of the other items covered in this book, there is plenty of subject material on paper items to warrant an individual book alone. The brief selection I have put together is just a small representation , however there ae some interesting items. The first row shows paper cups made by Fonda (USA) and a note set from Australia. Middle row features shelf paper made by in England by Cumbello and also from England paperware by Deeko. The bottom row shows a variety of paper coasters.

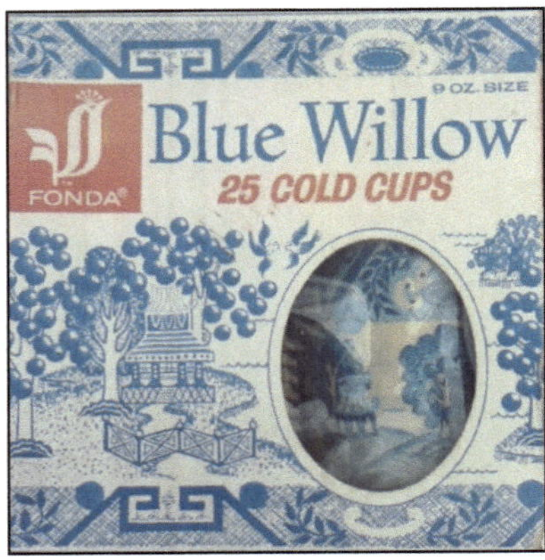

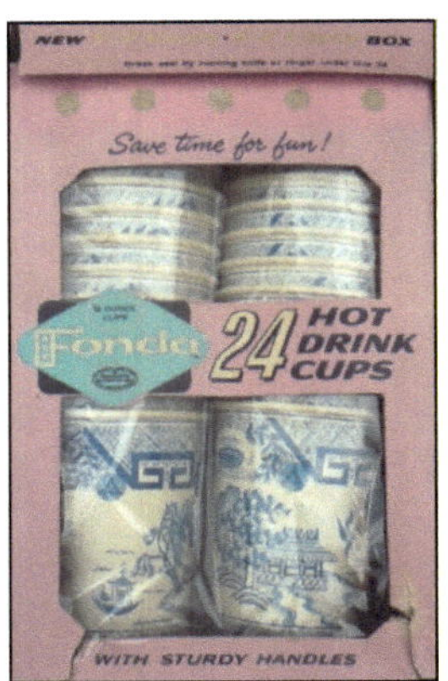

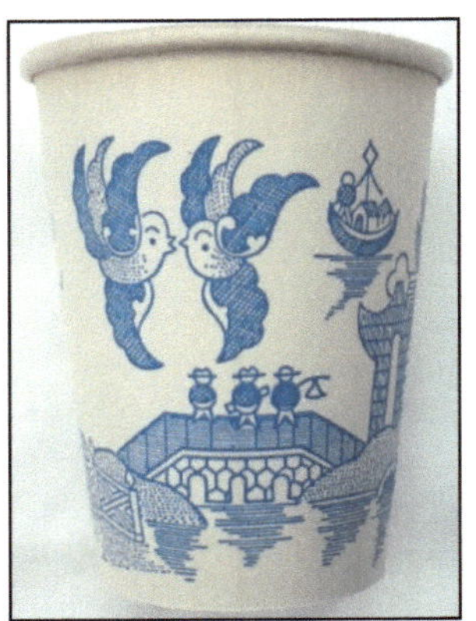

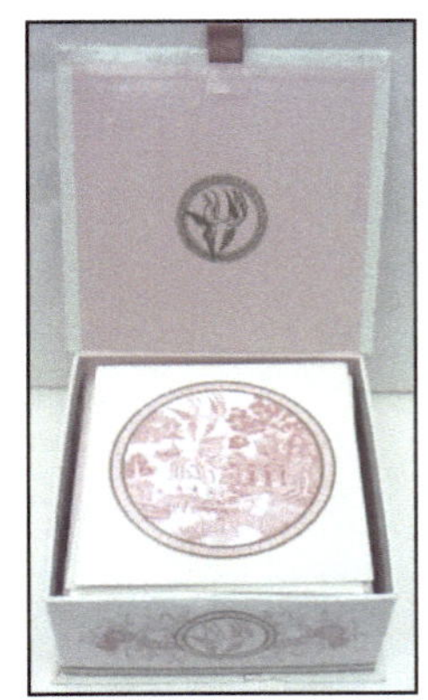

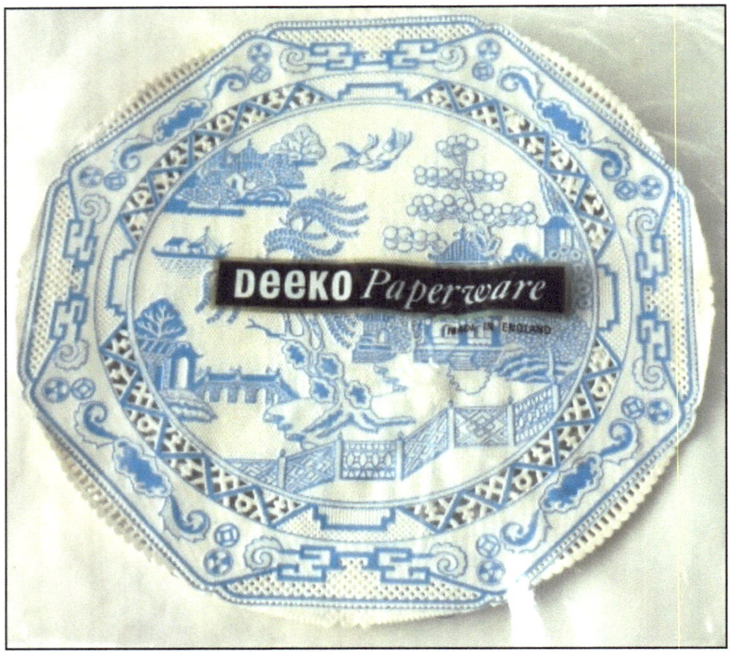

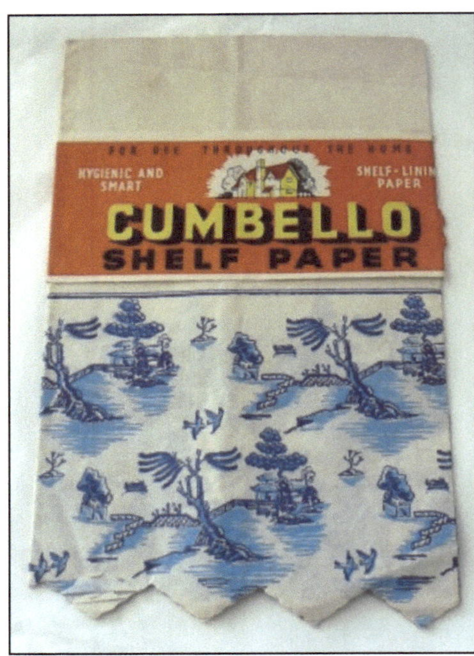

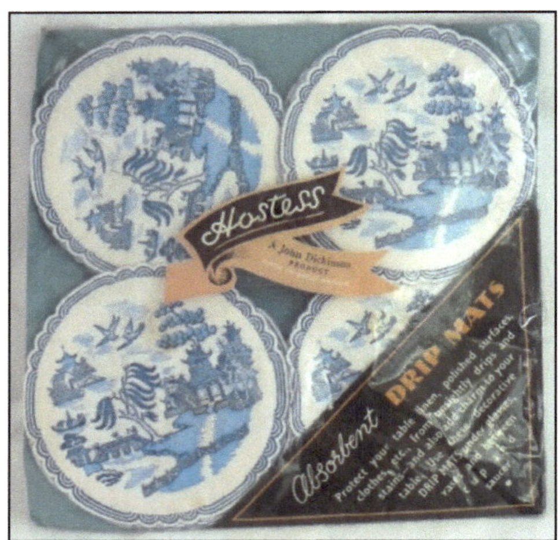

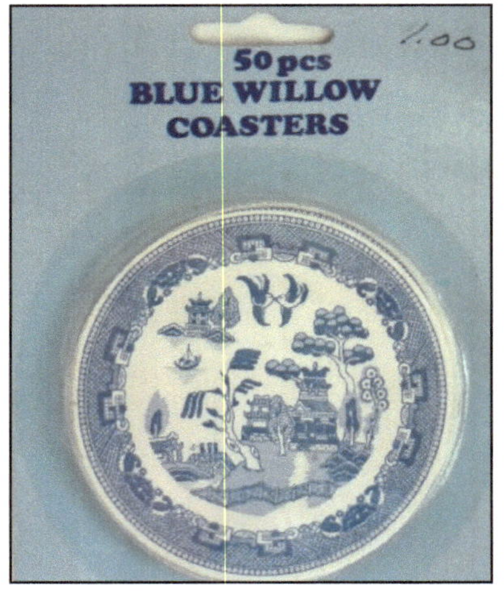

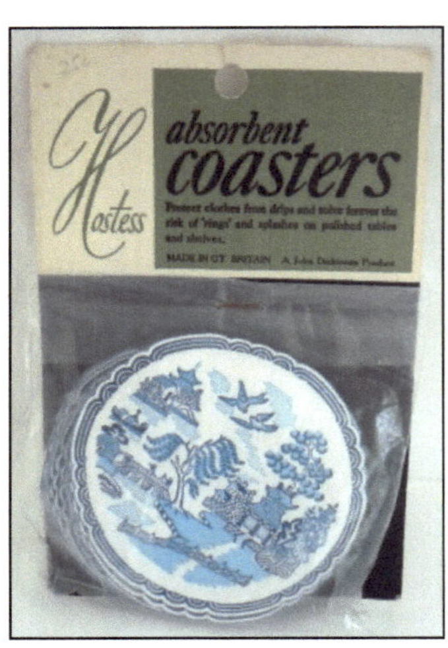

PAPER SERVIETTES, NAPKINS

With the Chinese inventing paper in the second century BC it is not surprising that they were the first to use paper as serviettes. There is recorded history of the ancient Greeks and Romans using serviettes. The Blue Willow Pattern has been used to decorate serviettes for many years, here are some modern examples.

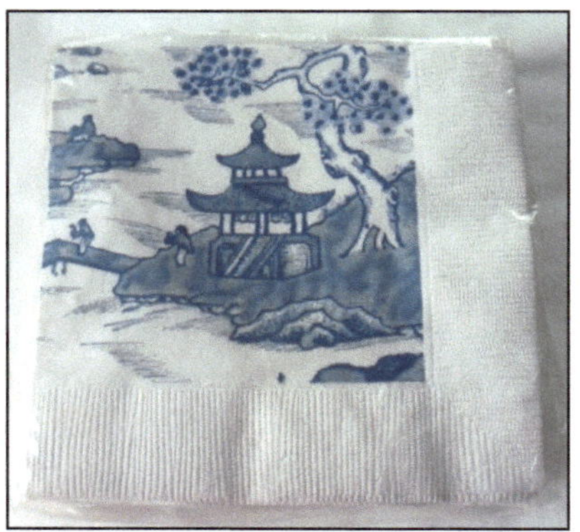

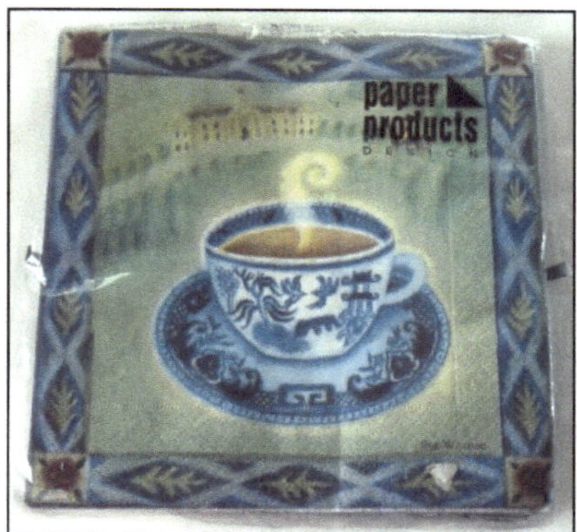

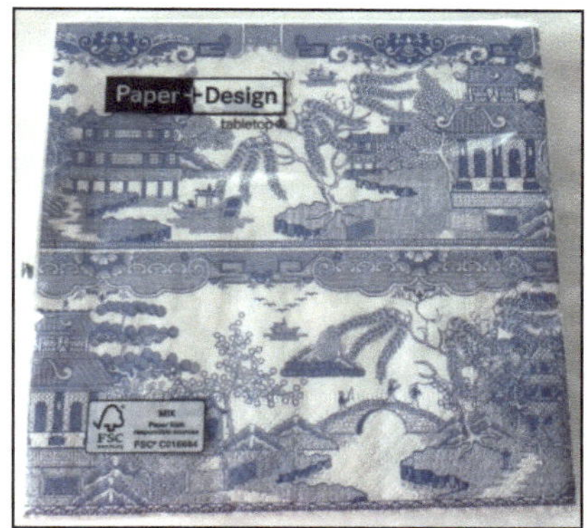

PLASTIC

Traditionally the Blue Willow Pattern is associated with ceramic items, but as you will have seen in this book already many other mediums have been used such as metals, glass, fabric and paper. A modern day material not often associated with the Blue Willow Pattern is plastic. There are childrens tea sets made of plastic, however pictured here is small plant pot where the white inner is made of a hard plastic and the outside is made of a soft blue plastic. The quality of the item is inexpensive and because of that many of them will have perished, leaving what few there are quite rare and now perhaps having some value.

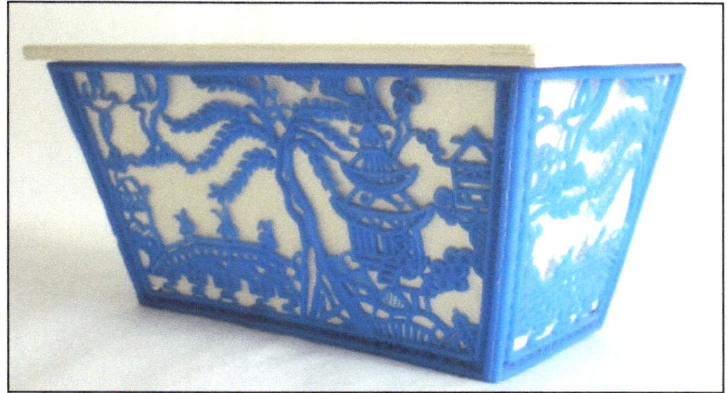

PLATES

You might be asking why I have a heading for Plates when there are so many in the book already. Well after putting all my material in this book and formatting it, I have ended up with a space that needs to be filled after the heading Plastic and alphabetically Plates fits the bill. I have therefore selected these interesting plates. The plate to the right has seen the Blue Willow Pattern varied to represent Maori culture from New Zealand and the plate to the left has subtle advertising for the Sherwood Inn.

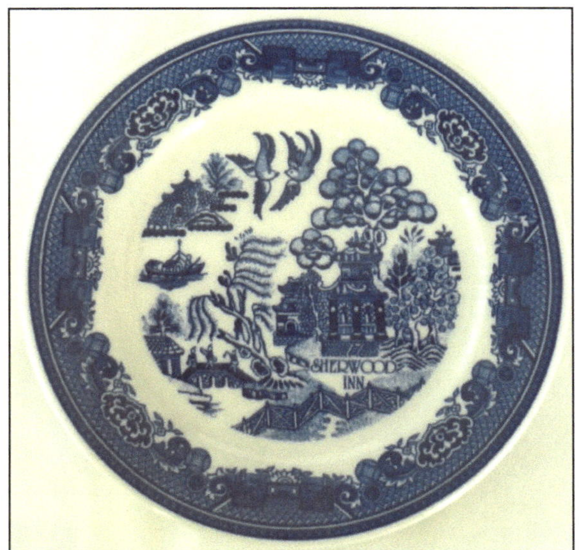

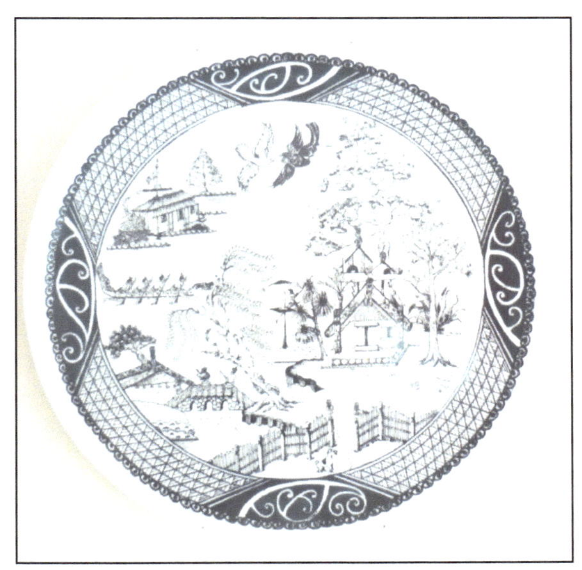

SPICE RACKS

An essential component to every kitchen is having easy access and storage to all the spices and herbs often needed for cooking. The word spice comes from the old French word espice. Aside from being decorative treasures, spice racks are also very functional. They keep the spices organized and shielded from dampness, light and heat. All the examples on this page are made in Japan, Many of the containers on the racks are already named for the herb or spice., some of the racks also display the Blue Willow Pattern.

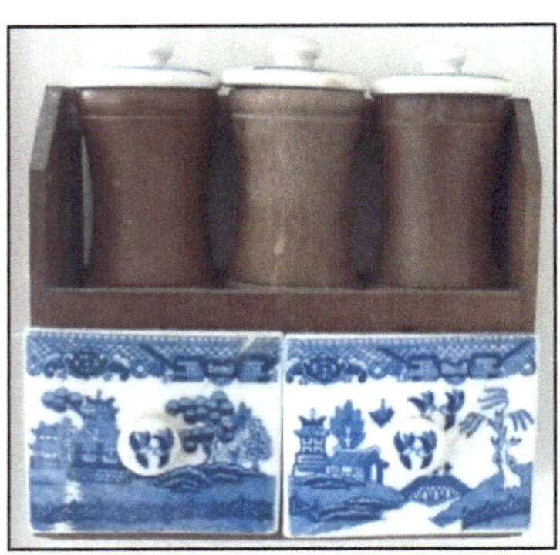

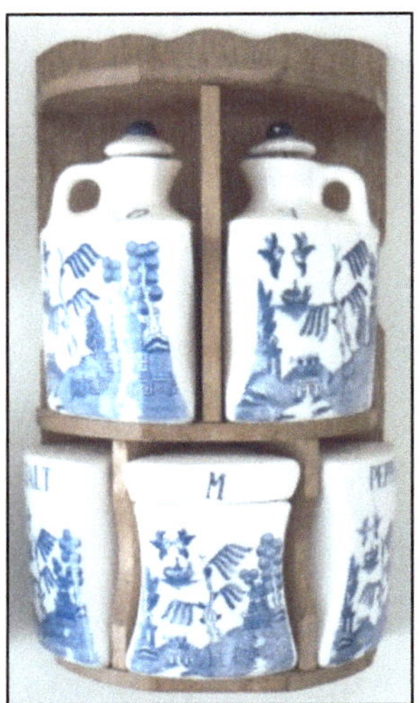

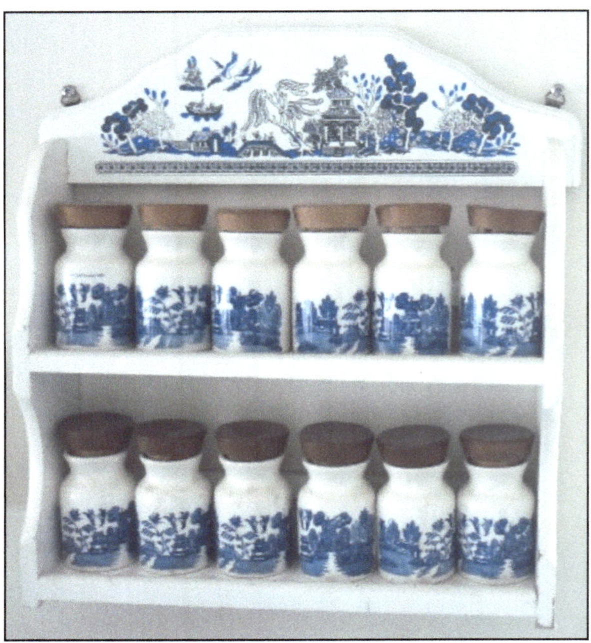

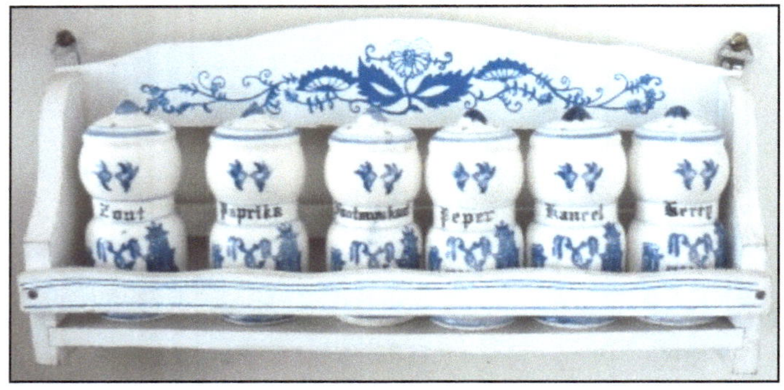

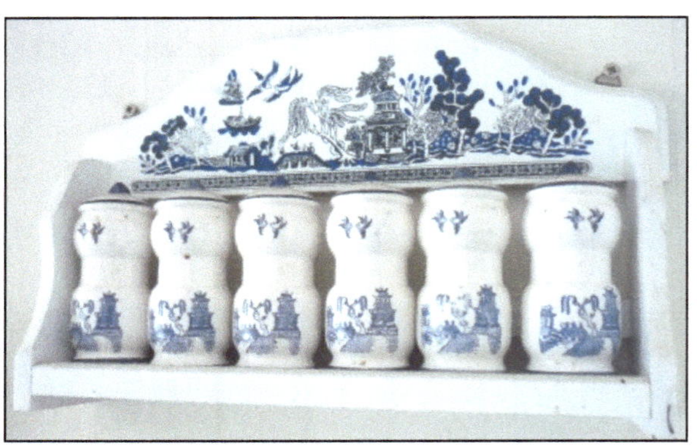

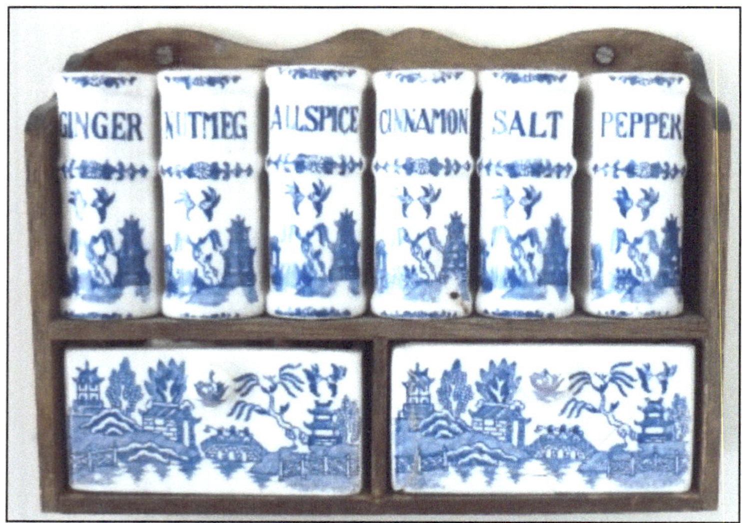

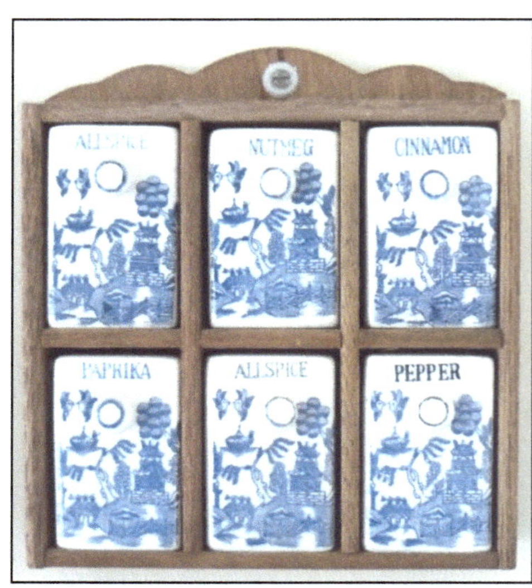

SHAVING MUGS

Pictured far right is a shaving mug which has the Parrot variant version of the Blue Willow Patter, the shaving mug to the left produced by Burleigh has the traditional Blue Willow Pattern .

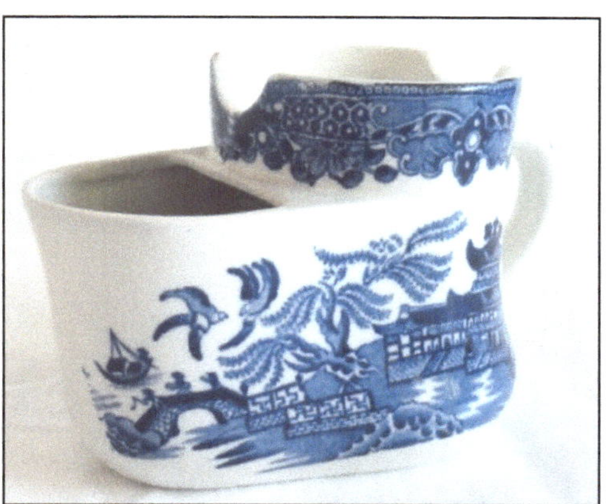

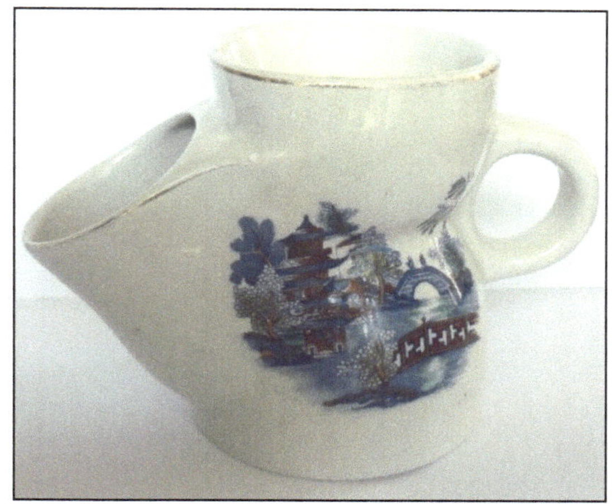

THERMOS (INSULATED) JUGS

There was a time when nearly every household would have a vacuum flask, or as it is more commonly known by the brand, a Thermos flask. The idea of a vacuum flask came up in 1892, but it was not until 1904 that commercial production was first commenced by the German company Thermos. The examples seen here are modern, with each jug measuring 15 inches in height. There is a reasonable chance that the Blue Willow Pattern was applied to earlier flasks, however with these early flasks having a glass inner bottle they were quite prone to breaking when dropped from any height. Hence once broken, they went straight to the garbage.

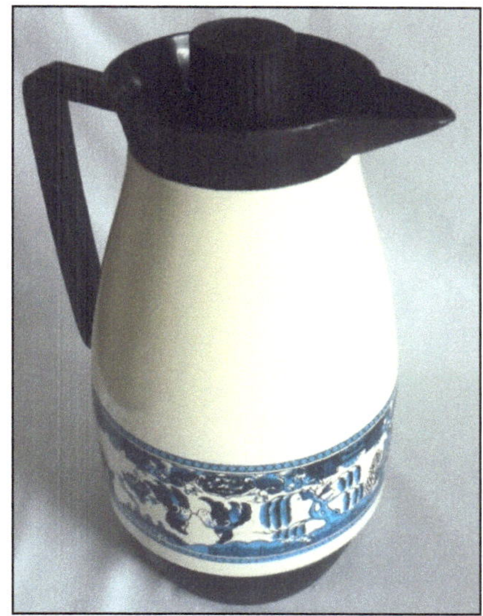

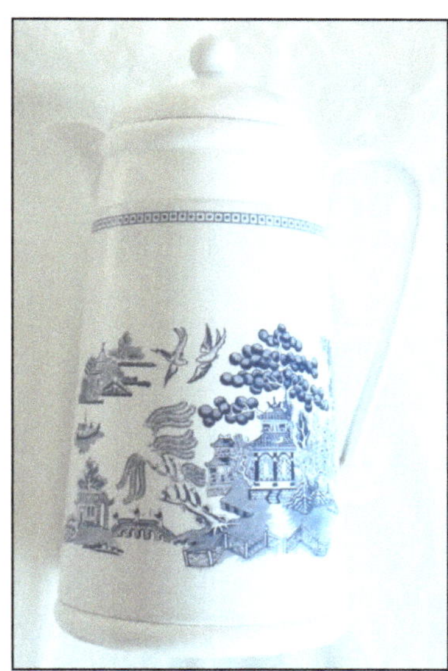

TABLE & HOME

The comfort of home living is helped by having the addition of the Blue Willow Pattern, here we have a circular rug and a brass tray which has been made into an occasional table.

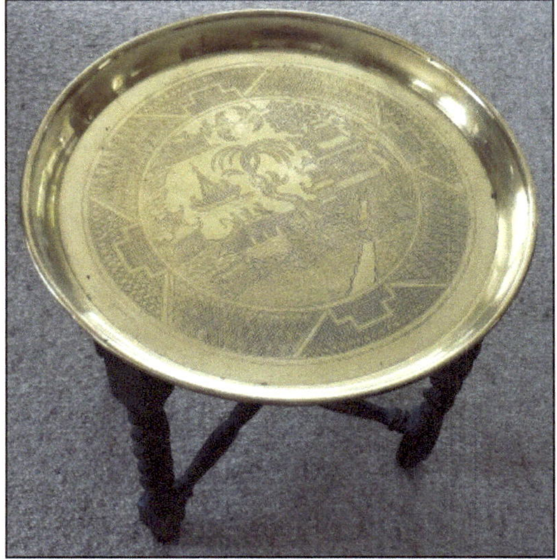

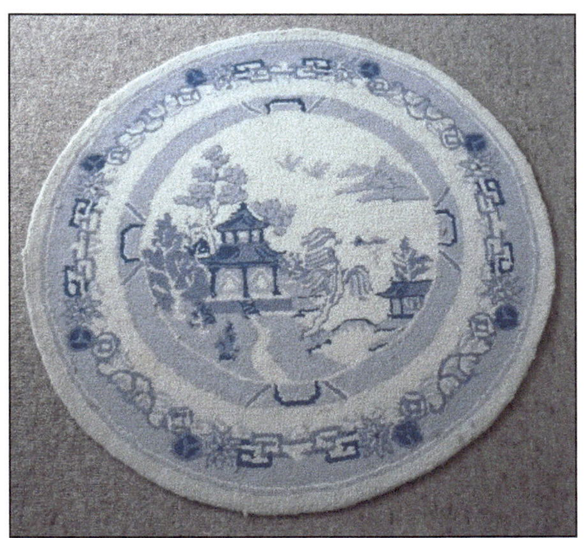

TEA CANISTERS (CADDIES)

Whilst quite a few canisters already feature in this book, the use of canisters particularly those made of metal to store tea is very popular. Needless to say with the Blue Willow Pattern being a regular feature on kettles and teapots, it is not surprising that the pattern has been extensively used on tea canisters. Modern tea as we know it originated out of Britain in the sixteenth century, since then, all manner of tea caddies have been used. The use of metal tea caddies though has often been seen as more practical than using ceramic caddies, indeed tea today is often sold in tin tea caddies. In addition to having a practical use, there have been a number of tea caddies which have been produced as souvenir items.

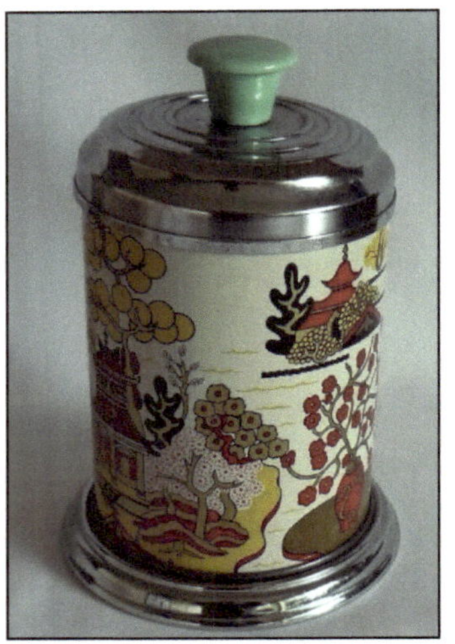
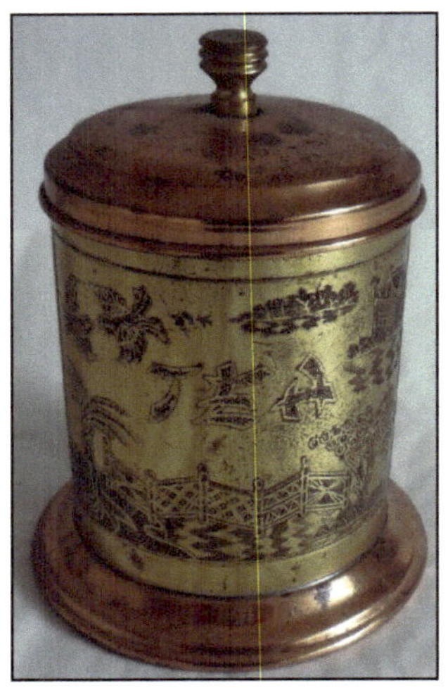
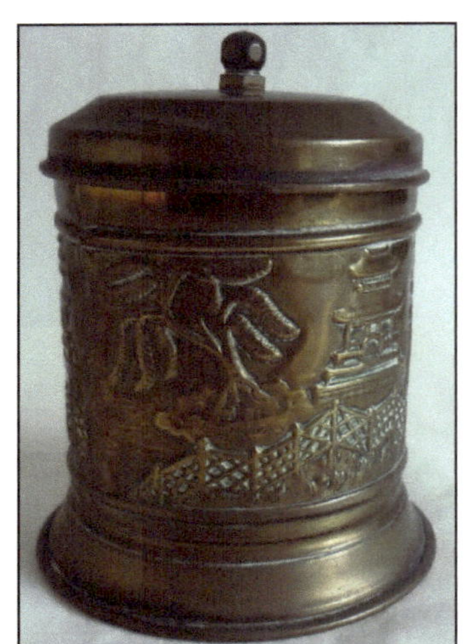

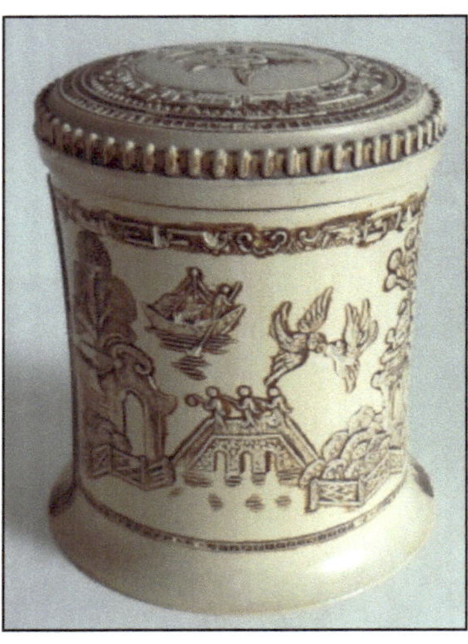
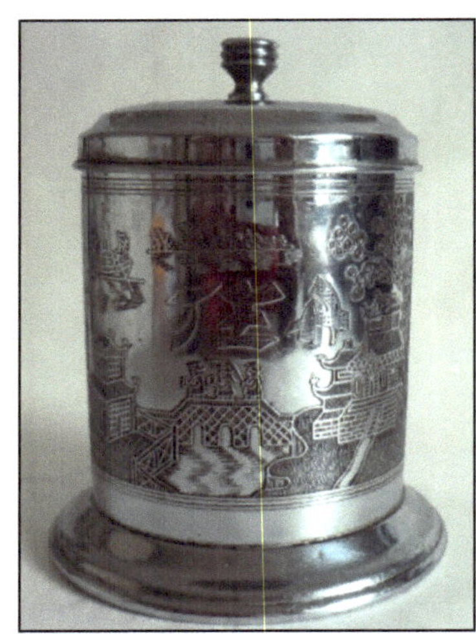
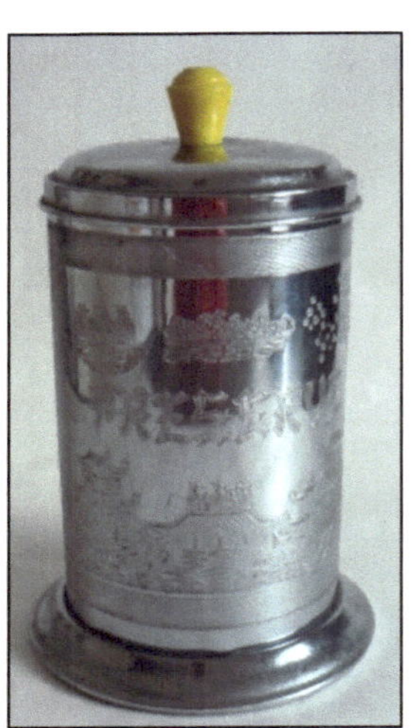

Pictured right is a ceramic tea caddy that has been specially made for Twinnings Tea of London. This piece which remains unopened and still contains the original tea was made in the 1970's

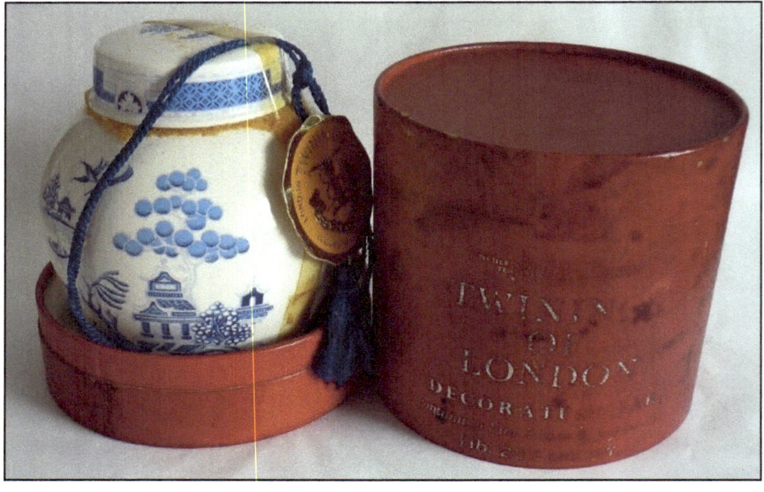

Time and the Blue Willow Pattern do not escape each other, there are many examples where clockmakers have used and still use the Blue Willow Pattern as a decorative clock face. In these examples the pattern has been used by American clockmaker Seth Thomas on a pendulum clock and British clockmaker Smiths on a tin plate clock. The application of the pattern to the Seth Thomas clock face is interesting as it has been applied on paper and lacquered.

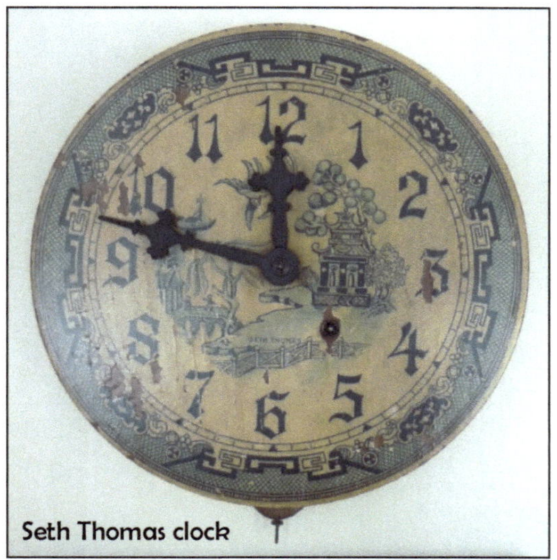

Seth Thomas clock

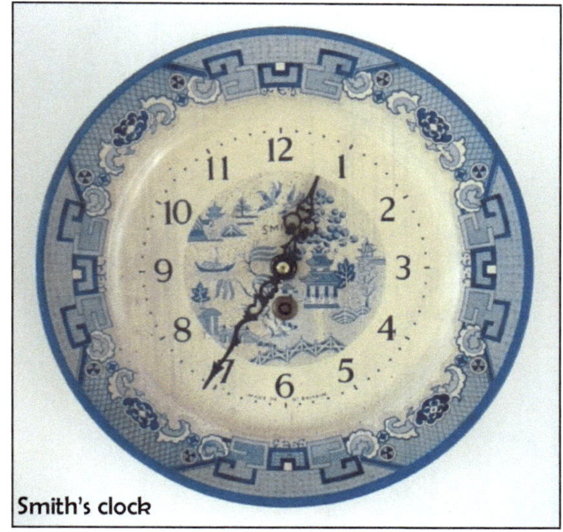

Smith's clock

At first glance this hourglass made with a supporting brass surround does not show evidence of the Blue Willow Pattern. However a close look at the top and bottom surface reveals the Blue Willow Pattern.

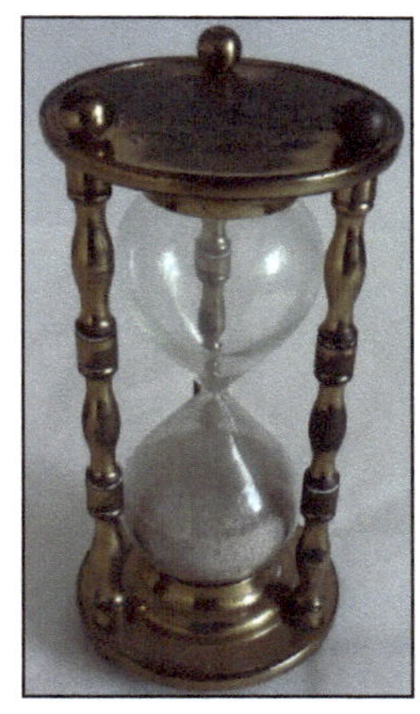

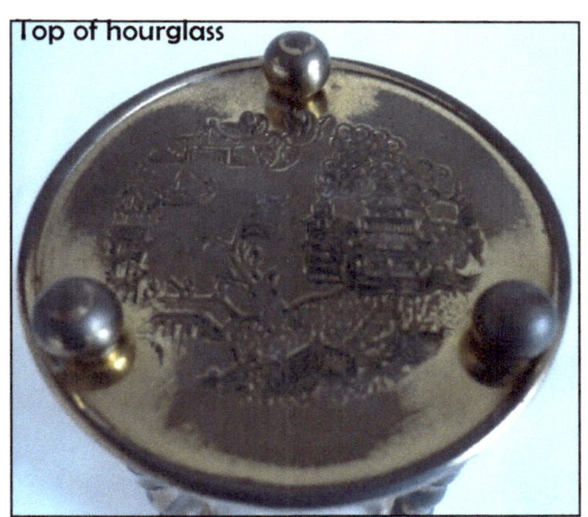

Top of hourglass

While not actually a working timepiece, I've included this wall pocket, it is pictured bottom right because as you can see the front of the pocket has a clock face being a representation of a cuckoo clock. I would have to say that this is an unusual piece, however it can be used as a wall pocket, though in this instant, perhaps more of a decorative piece. To the left is a modern mantle clock.

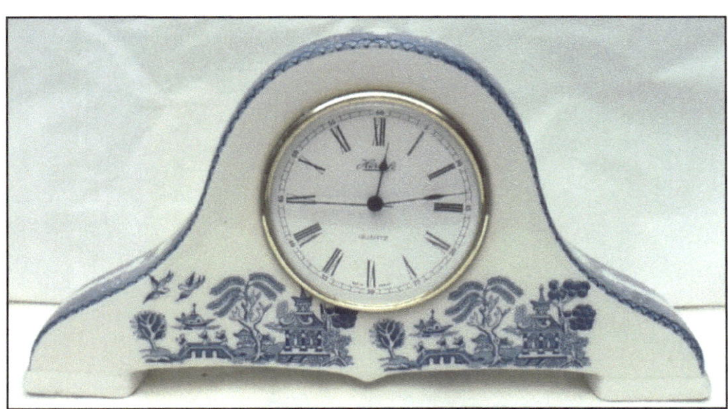

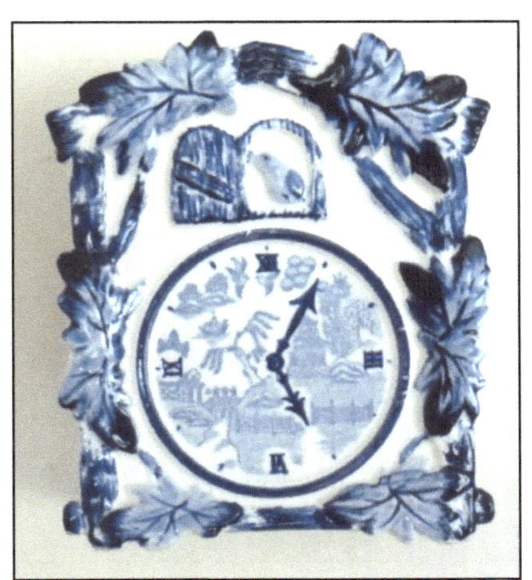

TINS

Over the past one hundred years and beyond, the Blue Willow Pattern has been seen on all manner of tins. Here is a selection of tins which in no way is representative of the hundreds, perhaps thousands of tins that have used the Blue Willow Pattern.

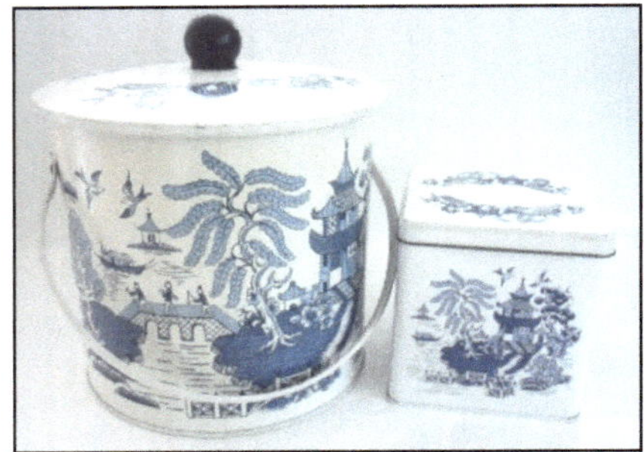
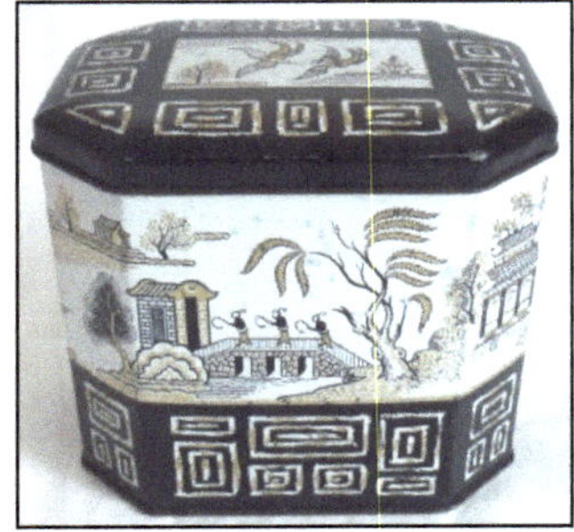
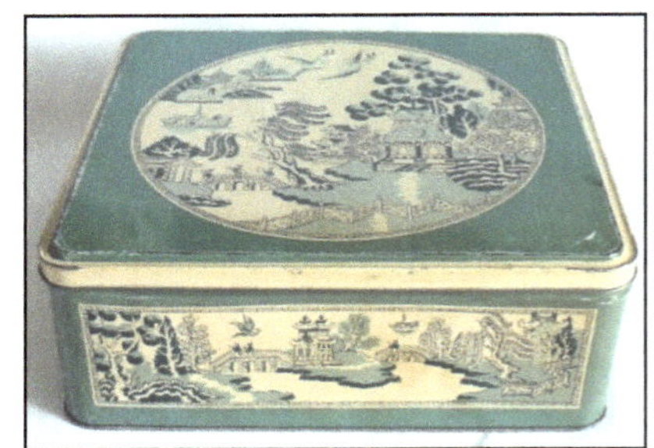

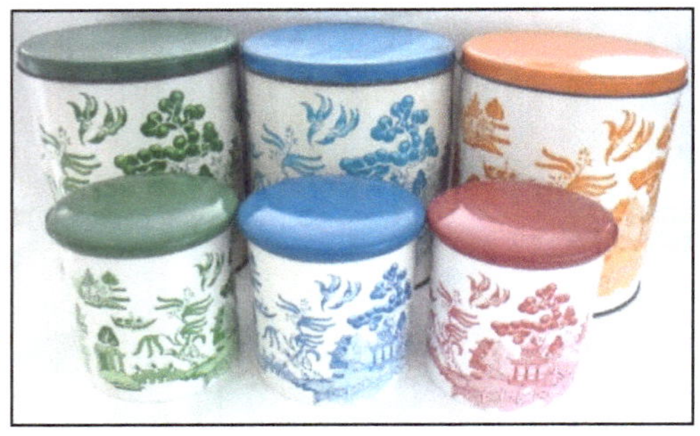
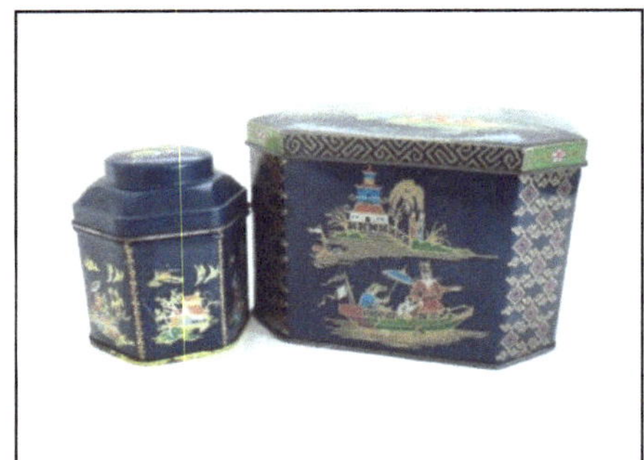
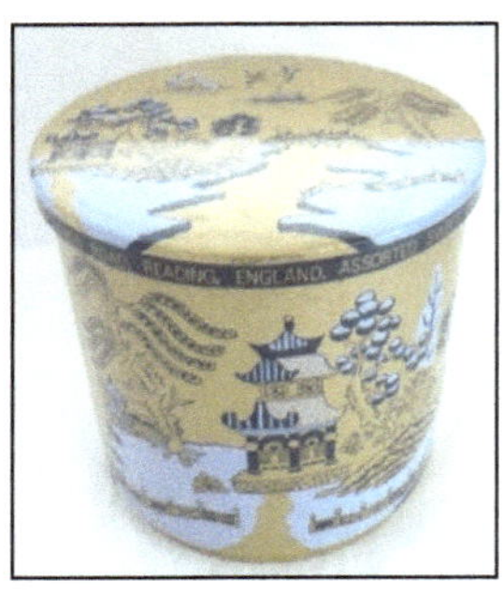

Pictured right and made by Willow Australia are a set of tins in miniature, the largest is around 3 inches tall. As a complete set they are considered rare and are now being held by museums around the world including the Sydney Children's Museum.

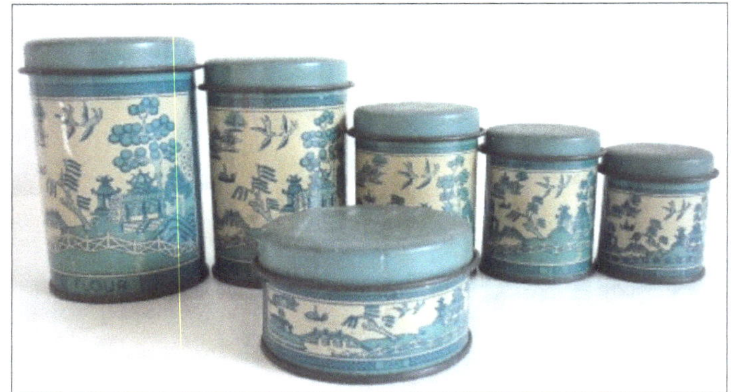

Pictured below, a rare set of tins on a rack which are used to store various spices; made by Willow Australia.

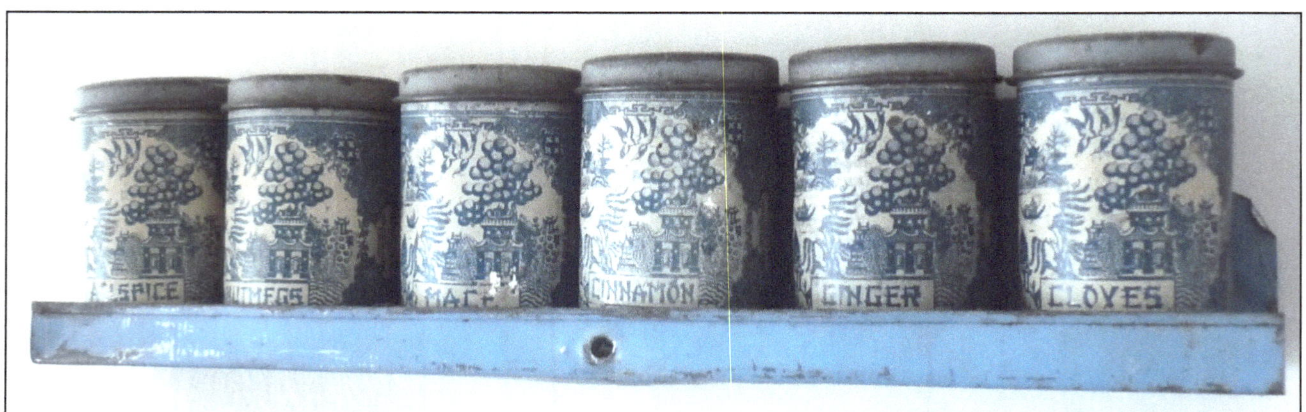

TOBY JUGS

The world of Toby Jugs is huge, so much so that there is a museum in Evanston, Illinois dedicated to displaying the numerous jugs that have been produced since the late 1700's. As you can see from these examples, these stout jovial fellows are both wearing a Blue Willow Pattern coat, with the exception of one which just shows the border typically associated with the Blue Willow Pattern. Nowadays Toby Jugs are perhaps regarded more decorative from their original intended very practical use as a beer jug.

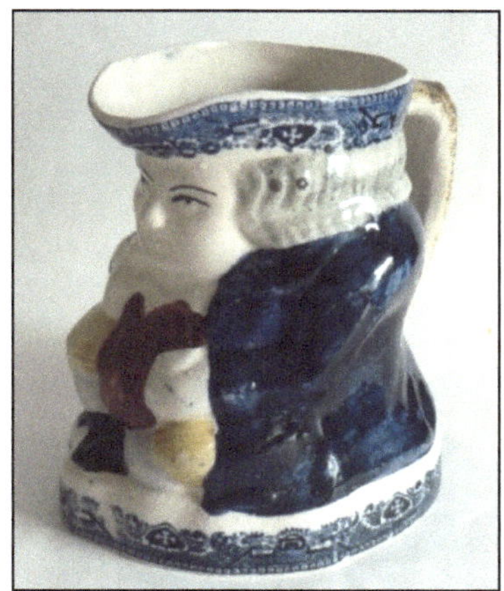
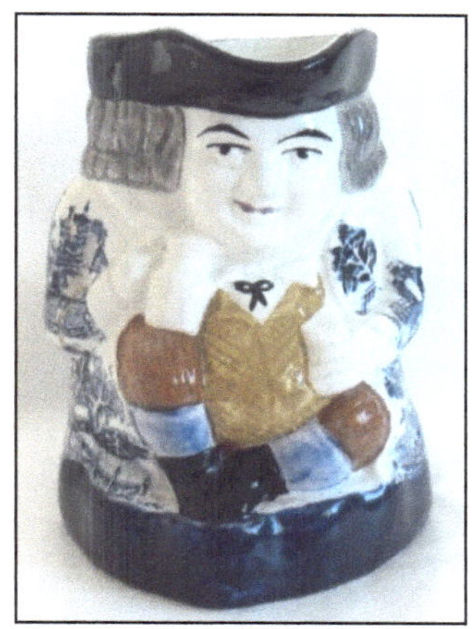
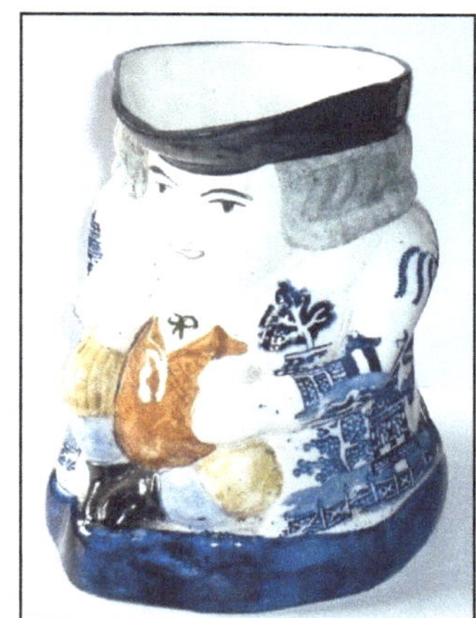

THIMBLE

There is a good chance that every household will somewhere have a thimble in it. There has been debate as to when thimbles as we know them today were first used, that said use of thimbles in 10th century England is evident and widespread by the 14th century. The early Greeks and Romans may have used thimbles, however no definitive evidence has been found to support this. From being made of plain metal and ceramic materials, thimbles have also been made from precious metals and adorned with colour and patterns. Suffice to say, there have been numerous thimbles made which come complete with the Blue Willow Pattern. Here are two ceramic examples.

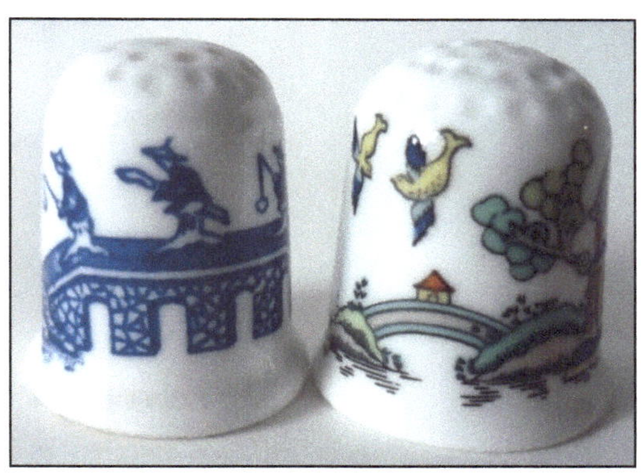

TRASH CANS

Yes, even use of the Blue Willow Pattern has not escaped being used on trash cans. Sadly time has not been too kind to these examples as being made of non galvanized metal they have succumbed to some rusting. That said, use of the Blue Willow Pattern is very evident. The open top trash can also shows the legend of the Blue Willow Pattern.

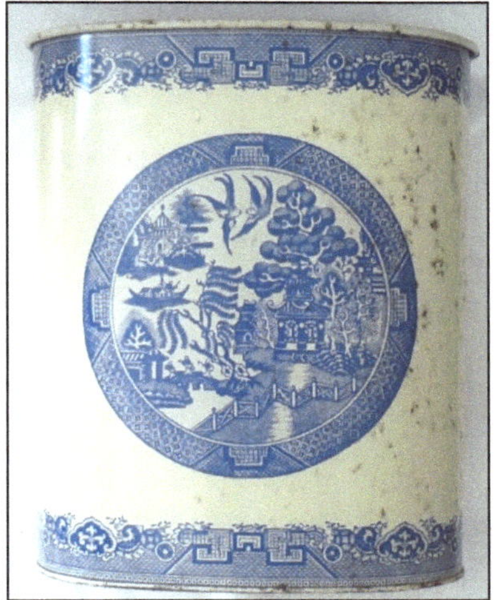

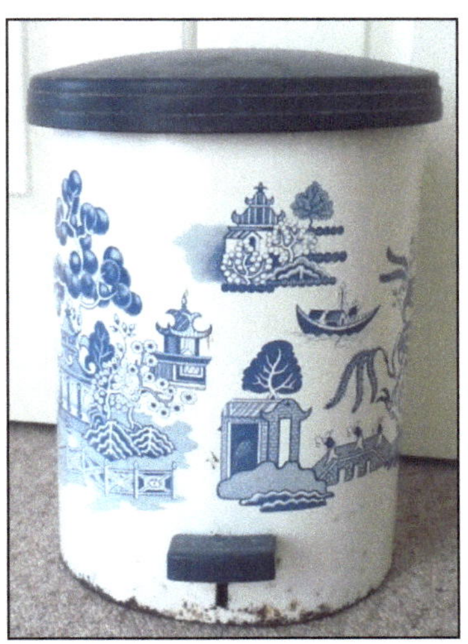

TRAYS

Since the beginning of the Stone Age, trays have been used to convey all manner of food, beverages and other items. The first trays created were plain and practical, though it was not long before trays made of wood were carved with designs and those made of metal, engraved or embossed. The creation of the Blue Willow Pattern has not been lost on trays and there are plenty of examples both old and current which have used the pattern.

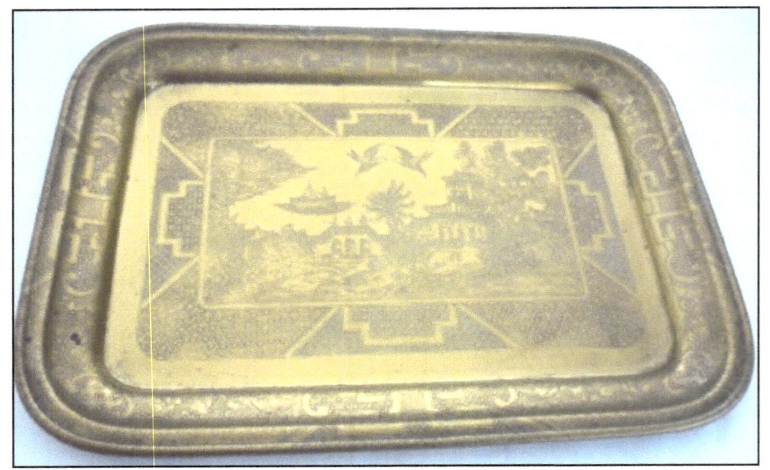

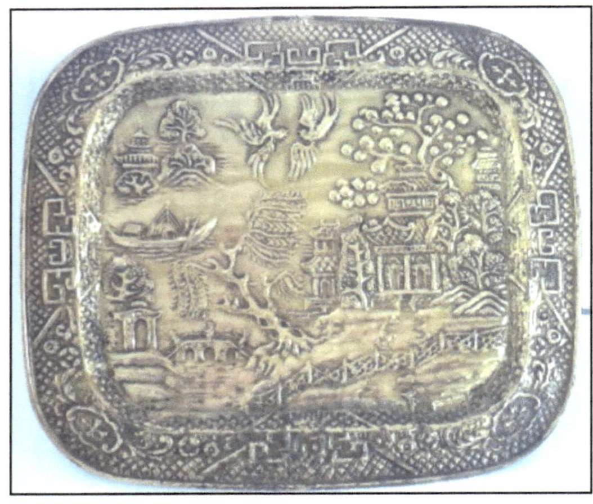

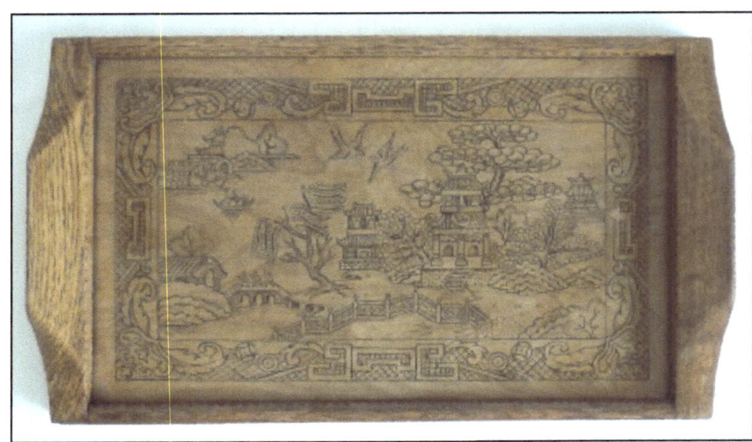

UMBRELLA

The word umbrella comes from the latin word umbros which means shade or shadow. Seen in Greek and Roman times, it was not until the 18th century that modern day acceptance of umbrellas prevailed. Apart from mechanical mechanisms, modern day umbrellas are very similar to those used in ancient Greek and Roman times. With the Blue Willow Pattern also appearing in the 18th century, no doubt there have been probably quite a few umbrellas that have been made with the Blue Willow Pattern. Pictured here, a modern umbrella held by Sarah which has 3 medallions of the Blue Willow Pattern.

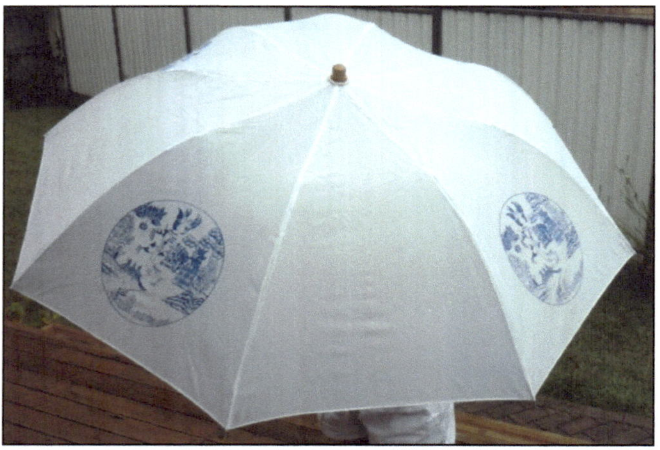

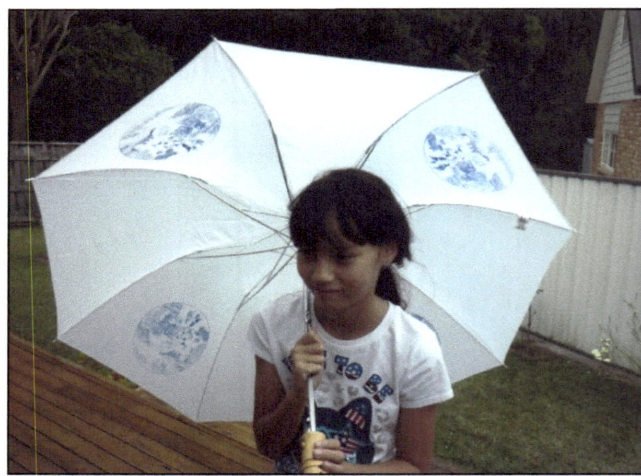

UTENSILS & CUTLERY

Here is a brief selection of utensils and cutlery that are made for everyday use. Whether you're looking for a carving knife and fork to serve roast meat, or servers for a salad, you'll see with these pieces that the Blue Willow Pattern has it covered.

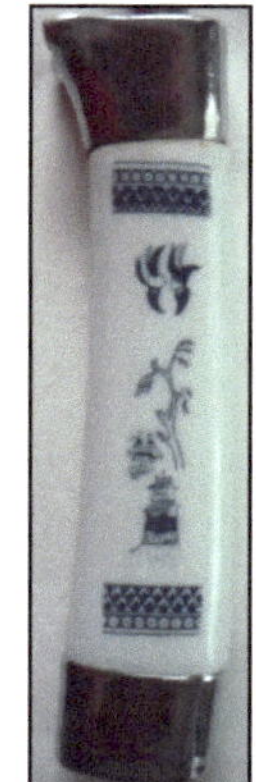

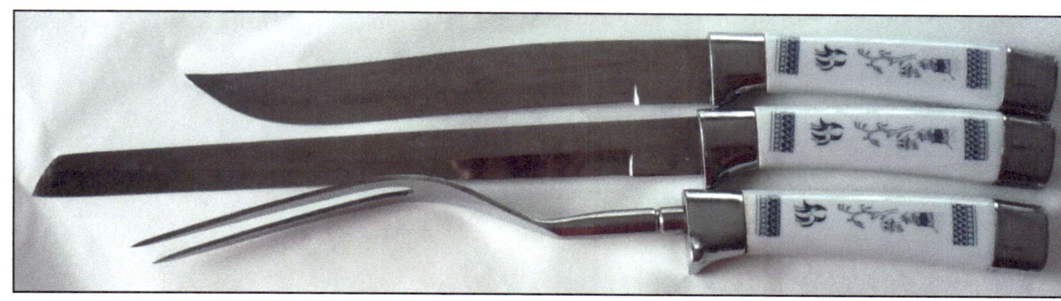

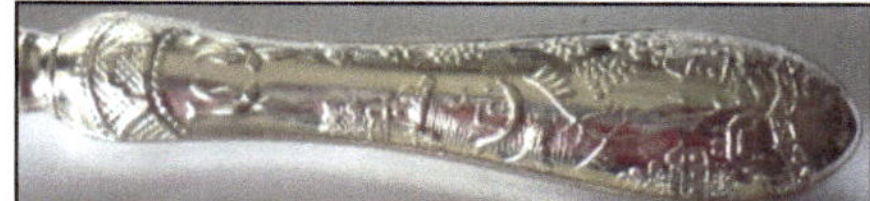

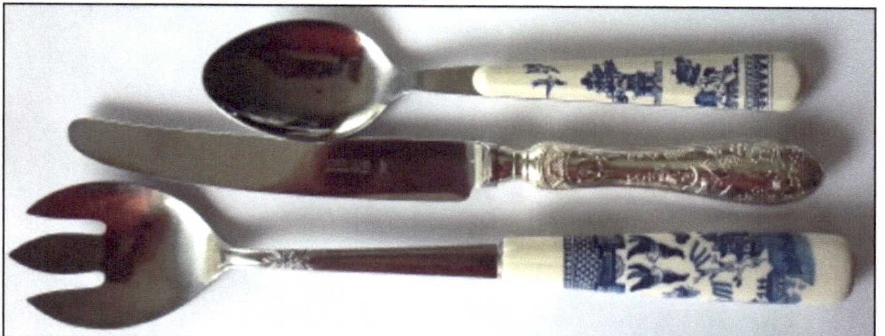

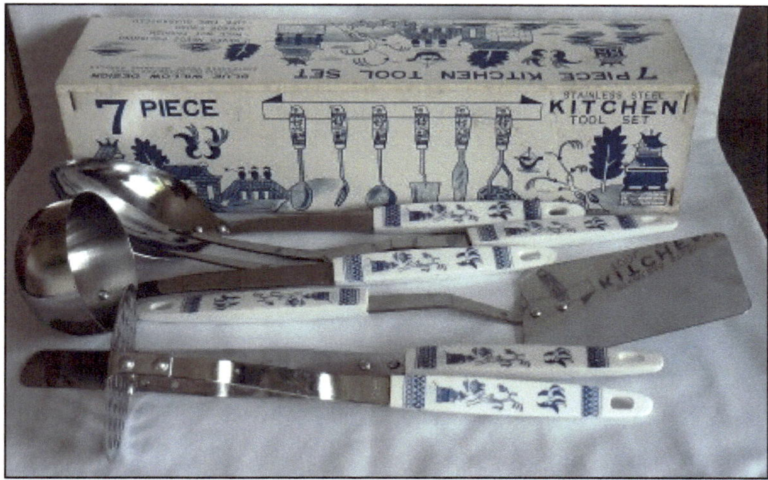

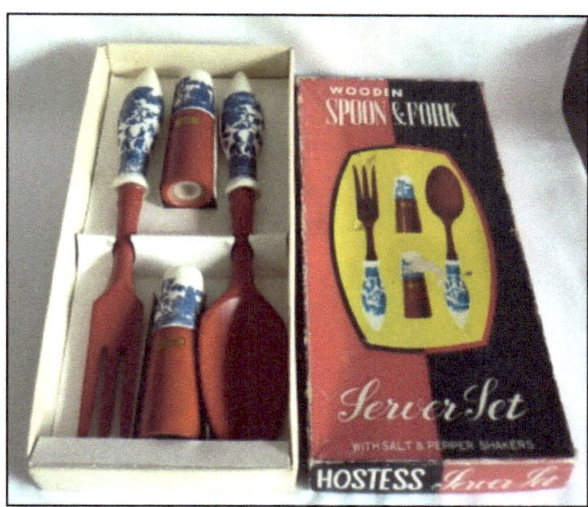

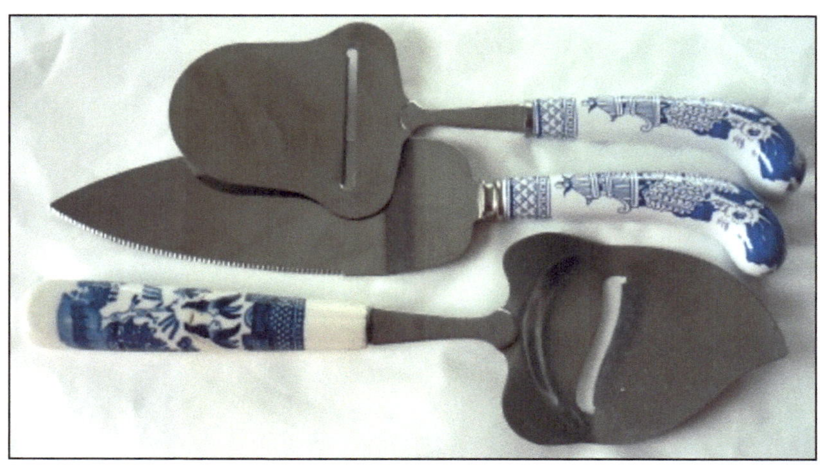

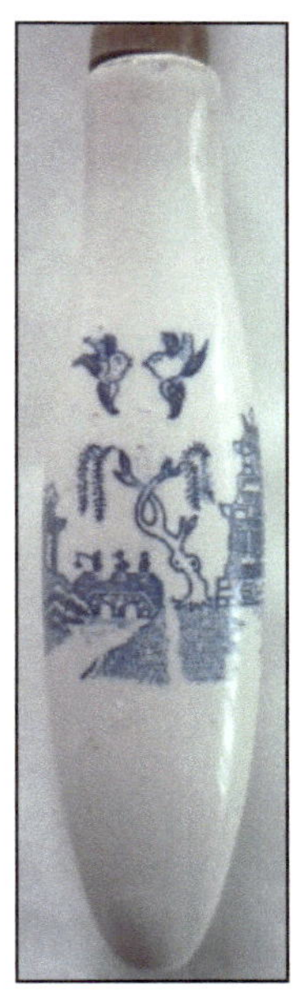

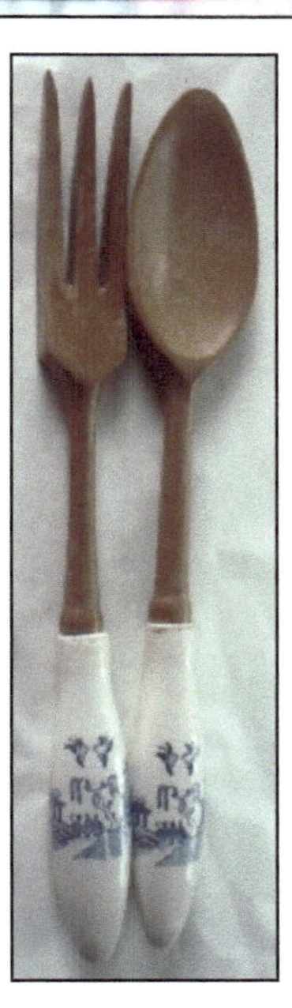

WALLPAPER

On this page you'll find a selection of wallpapers and wallpaper borders, all of which are from recent times, being made either in the USA or England. Some are currently available today, though their price can range from expensive if the paper comes from a boutique range or if in regular mass production a price comparable to everyday wallpapers and borders. With some of the wallpapers and borders, the Blue Willow Pattern is combined with other patterns and designs.

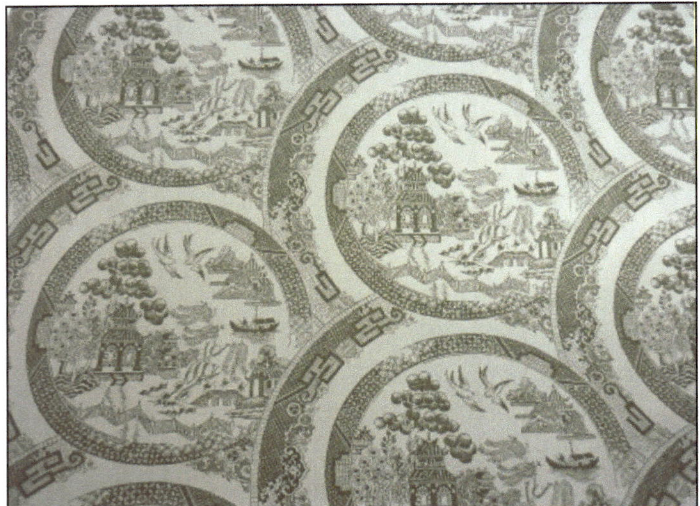

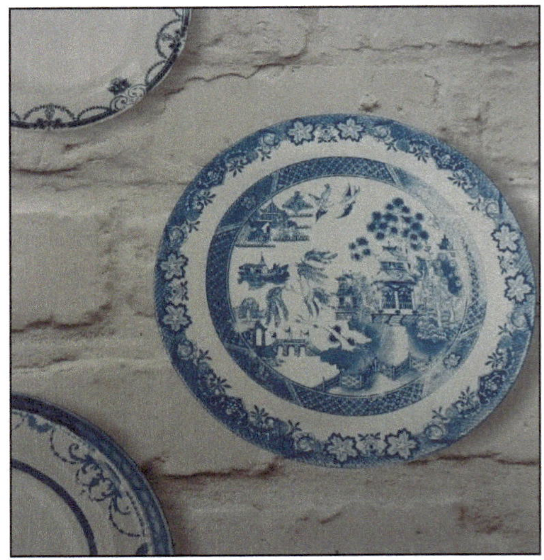

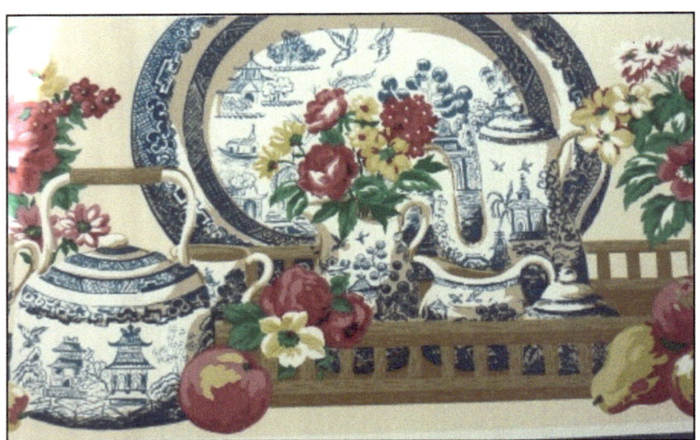

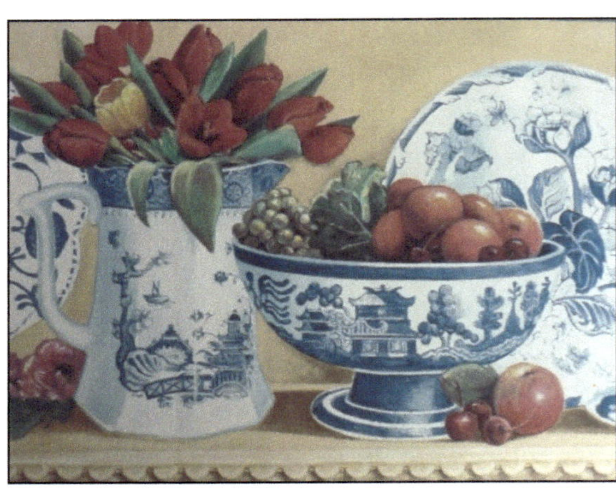

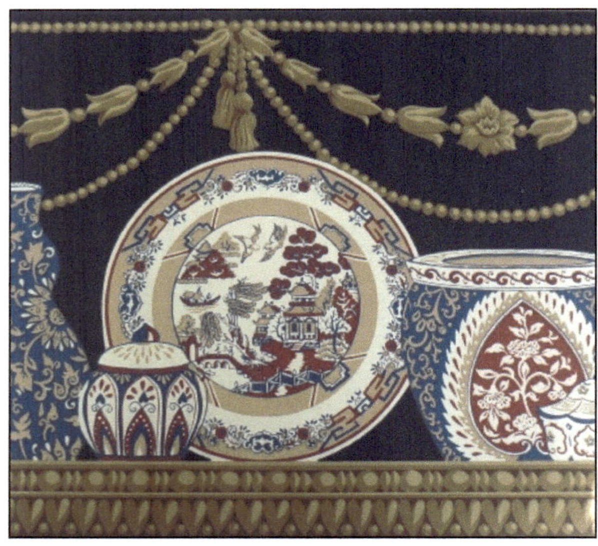

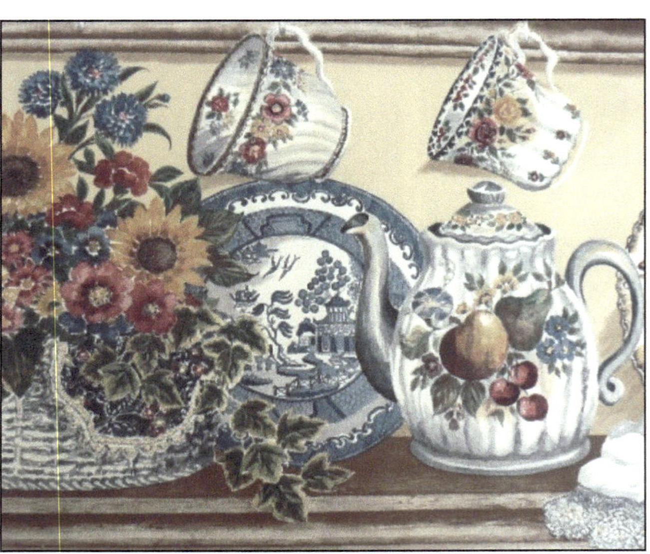

WALL POCKETS

Wall pockets as we generally know them were initially made of wood and had a practical use as a place of storage for candles and matches. While some were made of ceramics, it was not until the 1940's and well into the 1960's that ceramic wall pockets perhaps having more of a novelty value than practical were produced en masse. As you can see from these examples showing the Blue Willow Pattern while quite decorative they can be regarded as novelty. Often inexpensive when first sold, wall pockets are now becoming quite collectable as their numbers are reducing, as when hung on the wall for their intended purpose they have a tendency to fall and break.

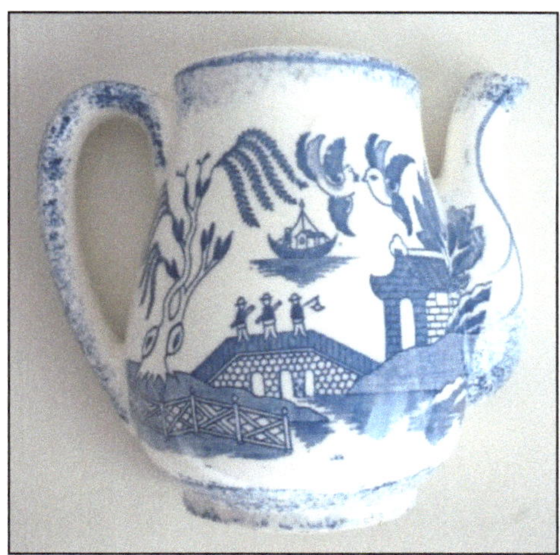 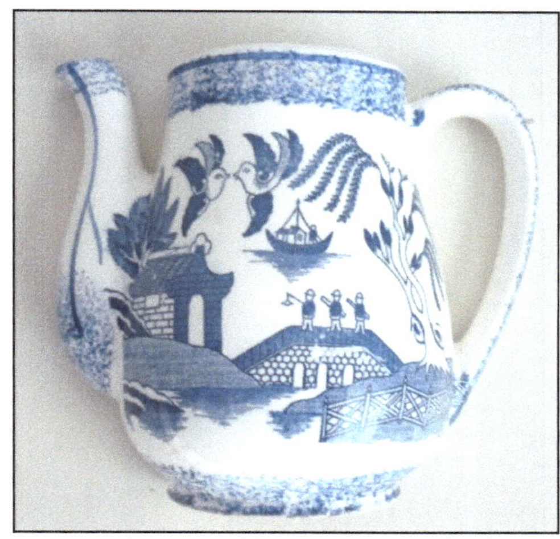 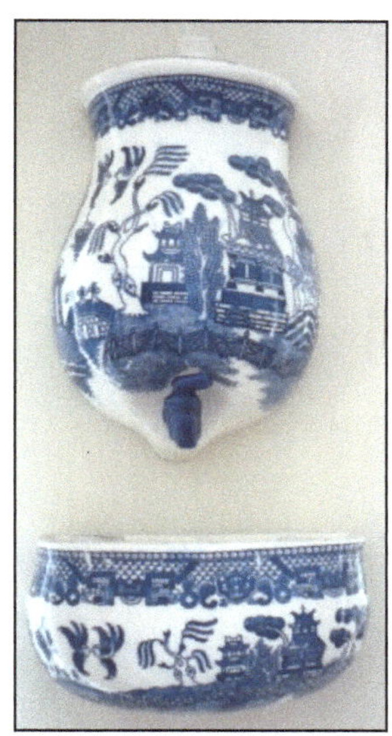

With wall pockets that brings to an end this book Blue Willow Pattern Collecting The Unusual. As you'll have seen throughout the book there are many examples of how the Blue Willow Pattern has been used to bring excitement and difference to everyday items that otherwise would have just been ordinary in appearance. I expect that there will be another book to follow this one, as like my previous two books, once you stop accepting entries, well they just keep coming.

My next book project on the Blue Willow Pattern is also going to be quite interesting and will look at how the Blue Willow Pattern has been associated with some famous and interesting people and places. The idea for this book came about by chance when I discovered that America's first President George Washington often dined on Blue Willow Pattern plates. Whether George Washington's life was influenced in anyway from what he saw in the Blue Willow Pattern and if he knew about the legend behind the pattern is up for speculation and debate.

Fast forward to Japan post World War Two, as we know the reconstruction and rehabilitation of the Japanese economy between 1945 and 1952 was led by American General MacArthur. During this period, ceramic pieces exported had the marking "Made in Occupied Japan". As you'll have seen in this book there is an abundance of pieces made in Japan, these ranging from our table friend the Snack Hound to those indispensable Wall Pockets. General MacArthur as well as having a successful military career might in some way be credited in causing the Japanese ceramic industry in producing all of those Blue Willow Pattern essentials and novelties, many of which are now mainstay collectables. So from George Washington to General MacArthur there is a lot of time to cover, I already have some great leads to follow, so watch out for this exciting book.

www.ingramcontent.com/pod-product-compliance
Lightning Source LLC
Chambersburg PA
CBHW042127030726
47599CB00002B/377